AF352357

For Sami Sikorski

First Edition

Printed in the United States of America
First Printing, 2014

ISBN 978-0-9907755-1-5

Dig That Book Co.
206 Royal Oak Dr.
Dickson, TN 37055
www.digthatbook.com

edited by Dave Wright
cover design by Dave Wright & D.C DeMarse

Furthest Agent

D.C DeMarse

[Do you have time to read all of this? Of course not. But I send it anyway, because you appreciate my work. This is mostly collage, save the beginning; poems I first wrote when I decided it was my job to do, mainly between ages sixteen and twenty. They lay buried for years in documents I discarded as the work of a facile, though nubile, but puerile intelligence; now I see a lyricism in them, have, enough, to put them together as a whole symphony of language. There is something here, my friend; there's always been. The subject matter weaves in and out, but the main points are stuck to, and I believe there was when I was younger a more linear pattern of thinking that developed, poem to poem. They work as a whole. The motif of the buildings, think of that if you bother to scour this. That I build and build here, both literally and figuratively. That's always been a favorite image of mine. Night, death, the mother, and the sea are the fourfold makeup of the "Sea-Drift" elegies. The mother is noticeably absent in this; death is noticeably present, as is the bending sickle of time, apparent even in the first suites. And the sea, the sea and the moon, tie together in various places in various ways. These were the first poems I ever wrote, my friend; and that they reveal something I have now lost, that is, something nearly pentameter, more serene, if a little outdated, is true. But these were the poems that gave me hope for working towards something. I don't know if I'll ever be able to write again. There's a mental draught, now; an immediate hesitance at the point I would have been able to sit down and pen something. I needed the pitch of that moment; I don't have it anymore. I hope you understand I've devolved into a rather awkward, abridged character of myself. It makes me sad, and I can only gloomily look upon this castle of words I've made, and wonder at a person I could have been, and once was. Therefore this is something most of all an epic for the individual. I like to think of it as: Beckett released from the stone, as an informant in a suit and tie, telling me of what HE saw, which is highlighted in quotations. To free him from the stone, I stop time, make it figurative, I stop the sea, I stop the metaphor, I cumulatively change the outcome of all---visions---to illuminate in the words as the sun does on the view. The sun's an image: so is the night, and death, and time, and the sea, and they all weave in and out sinuously. The 'outcome' here being, that that work was many different poems I wrote, when I first started writing, taken together, illuminating in their present shape some different- - vision. To stress. The image of the 'building' is appropriate here. Building on meanings, or a build of emotion that is also a cascade, culminating at the end: a lonely woman whose existence between walking from one to another room is in question. And rooms, rooms, poems-as-seclusions.]

"In the swamp, in secluded recesses,
A shy and hidden bird is warbling a song."

W. Whitman

[ABSURD BUILDINGS.]

The larger building looms-
-Over the other
Buildings: squat,
Gray. Minuscule,

Against the one
That looms. It is made
Of chiefest brick. It is a quiet structure-
-Of brick; quiet, docile to the point of seeming
Almost a fabrication: harmless,
Guileless, huge. It was built
At the outset, as a thing meant to bear the

Carvings: the carvings that we carve
To simplify: we
Frustratedly carve ourselves-

-Into humans. We do this. We carve out of
A complex, immortal clay
As a way to mold the weaknesses
Into what unevenly becomes uneven strength:
Deigned over always by the old disgusts
Of our lives
That we, and only we,
Had apprehended as clearly
As the knowledge of our beating blood,
At present, that is . . . before our end,
Starting blood
And clay together
And soon, into dust. We

Take all this and we squash it down
Into something compact, into-
-A flattering pretense, acceptable

And formal and external though
Still immortal as clay. Throughout-

-The metamorphosis, the relevance
Of the previous human is discussed-
-Between synapses in his/her brain,

And, the result is a perpetual motion
Of doubt, doubt of the virtues
Of what is now ourselves and what
Had not been rectified—aborted.

This is an attempt, yes,
To vindicate the self too soon;

Ourselves, drawn out with speech, now,
Explaining ourselves richly, as though
Before an audience;
Cantillated   as though all speech were psalm.

. . . . . .

These drams of the forgotten,

Good things about us, forgotten
By us. Now, but to be found
As scattered remnants bleakly
Across the page; to be made alive again-
-Strictly thru elegy. They are replaced quickly

With what we think is good
About us but is not, is

No reality of us. And then
Those former good things are-
-Happily dislocated from our palpable
Spirit, the kernel of who we are,

Reinforced by an acceptance of

This general self, from friends,
From enemies. This fake self, fake-
-Because general. Nonetheless,
We begin
To see it as who we are: another
Likeness made, thru

The weaving politic of one's selfhood,
Thru the fashionable-
-Ways to be good, the ways that people know
And all for the sake that others

May see this goodness that the victim
Of such change, mostly unconscious
Of the change, had
Seen in themselves, without needing
To change anything; for the sake that others-
-Remark that it is a familiar,

Identifiable goodness. Then,
At least he/she would know for sure. Wrong,

. . . . . .

Yes, it's wrong-
-To permit a larger building than
Ourselves can build, just to
Dismiss from us the need-

-To shatter our frustrations, frustrations

Like a toppling of brick; like a-
-Sense of smaller structures;
Like a building toppling shadow, dark and thick.

We think, we think of others-
-And their bitching ways, praise
Ourselves as being

The chiefest brother to grow divinely out-

-The hell of others' scorns. We

Hope the prey of our misled

Kindness towards our heady brains feels
No need for payback, but-
-Rather, throws away

That kindness we had just given it,
Just to give us an excuse
To be pissed off enough at this ungratefulness
To not alter ourselves, warp ourselves;
Having now an excuse based in anger
Towards ourselves, we then would
Understand clearer the crucial dissent
That we originally promoted,
Using the cause of our alterations against itself:
Cause, coiled around us in an indirect anger
Directed at who we were. We could-
-Not handle the guilt of warping our own personality
Again; even if we could,
We wouldn't do it, being too weak, too tired
To change

Ourselves twice. That is, we would not
Pay back that self in us not known,

Who gives us mysteries to solve, yes,
But out of something else,

Something else not kindness, but
An obligation to the larger building,

The larger building, containing

Other people just
As haunted by the things
They owe their heads; peopled
In their heads with people-
-Who lent them things.
Things they cannot give back,
Not yet. Imposter. It is an
Inability to reach a closure
Regarding debts

To one's own spirit that professes-
-A really troublesome ownership of things

That are not theirs. It is a SOUL that is not theirs,
Not yet, yet theirs for now, until

The same vicinity in which-

-The other people dwell in debt,
In poverty, in exquisite poverty

Becomes where they dwell too. And,
They find themselves living-
-In a ghetto of the mind,
With others who were as-
-Affected by their marasmus, since
It is, we are all affected, equally and together,
By this marasmus. This

Is horribly possible. These-

-People, these people living
With nothing in their minds,

They strain their abiding conscience

To act to reinforce the positive
In others,

Others who in turn will act

To supersede that other's seeming goodness
With compliments that lay like heavy weights

Upon the faults of them. The-

-People who receive
The compliments, hem
The boundaries
Together, closer,
Closer together, despite that that

Longing for another person-
-To keep what they had given
Without paying is the same
As longing for a building not so tall;
With less, yes, with less-

-People in the head to muddle
The people who
Are already balls-deep
In thoughts
About themselves, caught-
-Up in that, that is, the
Insidious implications
Of being owned by other, hideous,
Talking spooks who whistle

In the ear. They feel obligated
To accept a closer vicinity-

-Out of fear of losing validity.

They care, too much, about

The neighbors on their floor,

Who shout, and so then
Have to close the door,
To keep the labor
Of their argument-

-From proliferating hateful,
Regressive though vehement things
Of privacy, thru
The walls to
Other people who may

Hear it and then comment on it

To the other hearers of it, if
There were others. The calls

Of people in the head
That differ, one to the other
Create friction: live wires never dead,

Merely, it is alleviated, yes,
With time in bed-
-To sleep on situations, yes,

On situations, yes, the situations

Of buildings that they think
Taller, for the presence of themselves: they

Would not feel this if there were not

The higher shelves, the shelves above,
Where people live, and live, and live,

And cling to what
They cannot give: to what

The shorter, smaller buildings have:

. . . . .

Those buildings, tinier,

They play a minor/major part in what
The larger people in the buildings think,

Think, yes, of themselves

And their own shelf of understanding:
Including all, to those who live
In the same building; and yet there is

Always information pending, always
Larger people in a longer building; there
Will always be information
To be given, even
By the folks upstairs, later.
A higher floor

Will beat its shadow on the lower floor

And we can only understand the heat

Of that shadow, yes, a figment
Of veritable thoughts we thought before,
Before, before we knew-

-Of shadows higher up,

Higher buildings, higher seemings,
Yet nothing ever is concrete except

In dreams-
-That wage a solipsism,
A telling of the meat of one's pure self

In dreams, where seeming is concrete,
And everybody's infinite. The

Highest building is the highest dream,
And so then limited, dumbly cruddy. Cruddy,
Without things to reach, to reach.
We reach, so that
We might embellish
The shadow, make it deeper, relish
What we have, and feel-
-Not so limited, and so then lighten up
The shadow, just a bit,
With some talk of the absurdity of it all

I. A JOKE ABOUT LEAVES.

    Tap wristwatch with index finger looking at it to see if it
works,
Fiddle with cog on side, take
        the same fingernail to nose's bridge, see glassy
Clouds momently, fiddle with cog—
            On side, no luck. An understated second-
hand
Is consumingly quiet, realized, if in place. Good morning. Itch—
          Neck, then cozen a brittle, shapeless
Beard, then leave sainthood.
      Then wake up fully so as to resume the clonus,
Instruct my hands to stare at the objective
    Control on the other side of the room: take off a few scales
          From the vision. Whatever ancillary
Whispers in my head shoo off soon as I like
Drink coffee and hurl the western star
            Back to the planet's other side.
And find time broken. For it is HE stranded life here for fathoms
in this place
        Of leaves, and it is where they are frozen
In time, and azure waves passing
Between each other to crash an infernal age of this hit like
marbles
      And froth too: by yellow moon's
  Charter will make considerable
        Tempests of a soul's clockwork: and for to make
it

                    Sing fathoms itself, the age of the boy: to
Shore in waves, carpet vessels
 Of content, wires, where rain meets the
 Brick of rough prizes: of a valid as deep as the sun's
            Absurd buildings: and as well the appareled night
                    In its folds of cloud
            Speaks nigh thunderous. Interrogatorily,
                    Remarks came, left, sped up to get
                            Back in parentheses here,
Like a laughter of the sun again behind its clouds
And to leave again the wiser storm, HE say. To this day, HE
            Has told me time. It is
                    Quite sobering, actually
When I shall build my own recitative
            And shorn the special parts that
 Brought me there, give up you wires;—

 Belated simulacrum, return me
            To the concentric eve of words
        Of my becoming. Speak it here
    In remarks-
    -In studious, melancholy rooms, alone:

Things are consumed at angles, the
Colossus of the mask, whispers soft as new grass
At the hilt of spring. I am now arched into the pace
Of that dusty, nameless timepiece—
Air conditioner of some kind humming
Sometimes works and then not

   Four cups and a mug on the table
            —Next to the bed. The undeniable
                    Picot of strange depth traveling down
Into some pathetic HELL strange it would be found

16

In this dark hovel these epitomes of the personal
Stacked like books without a shelf:

(Clenched in tweed about my wrist
Works the watch a tidy trail. The brass bowels
   Quake and leaks from there a humble hiss:
Locks quick—his steel in bores
                    Then curls round notches,
Absently he twirls the wheel of his welded rail
         As do all watches.

                    Watch: give your rations to the EARTH
      See—the seeds of time—grow, indelibly, with
Your work. How—the Incredible Year
            Holds many years—progresses from them all
      Then rolls another year another call
To test the soul and rest new fears
—That each man feels.

         Does watch decide to shift his bolts?
                    Men lift words—from former throats and
History repeats, as do the actions of the watch.
         So is the watch born whole born
Individual, and yet
      Whose dashing spool
And metal spoke
Turn thoughtless, visceral, within,
 Just as—the circling organs
Within a man—do work, and
Only underscore—the other body that is will
                    That is free thought?

         Men—certainly can—decide their chores—and trust
            Themselves: their

Individual behalf, that tells
         What way is best, tries to strike
         The answer: a little cell of freedom never taxed—
         By the fate, that drives
     Mechanics, of the wheeling of the watch.

The chronicles of men, and our events,
Flute out like the snapping of an hour—
         —With the simple turning of the screw,
   The watch, efficient, makes its cue—endows
 A few more minutes—for man's troubles—
         And proves his power—of all manner struggles.
      As none of us could reach our ends
Without the time—thus time, commands
Our end.)

 What speaks, though, tell me what speaks to shake
   So plaintively goddamn it in shelflessness:
  These sheaves of waves
Leveling the book: that carry,
  Sleek and trim crazily upon the—
         Azure vault, that is, some sea's oneness:
within
         Its dives is dark and black?
      What speaks so perfect
       In wave, that—sudden breaks,
Breaks, loses form like you know
Upon—coral isle—rock—
And, what hiving there communicates
Serenely in the eye—and will again—sandwiching a view—
By which, its user, a young boy, gazes
On all the burning buildings, as
        Though asleep …
What speaks the eye, which cannot know

The user's valid deep?

What broke the souls that lost?
Rather, what reassurance did everybody lose when
Loyalty—was tossed, as are tossed
                What worked before, and now do not?
   Loyalty is altered as alters the age for
Each vice and each falter
            In time will be played—

In time, will stem reasons to folly, to change,
To build to perfection one must cover past rights—

—And yet, before the folly, was loyalty
                —to the old discoveries—the minds
And statements of formal and religious men
In formal suits—were seen as truth—
Yet now dwindling. To bookish rumors
For the ones who've lost—weaker comes their sound as
Pass the years tortuously—sneering out of weakness
Under the hemming
Beam of relativity. It stretches forwards
Like a fence across a field.

Or, to His name affirming life,
        Loyalty to that, for it is God, I suppose.—
That opens to the caring, that works for the compassionate.
 But no, not now,
No compassion
Comes now—it is late for that.

Fate has already acted
On the World—and it is grim, and black—
As the depths of the sea.

(We our nearly extinct things, ignorant and arrogant
Things—who think not on how we
Impede our own and failing future as we waltz. Yes, along.
Through attacks, we waltz.
And attacks the more—we who wearing our
                    Expensive clogs and cravats—we step
 From moment to moment—never believing that
We are leaving a Footprint of some kind behind. Not looking but
Mesmerized: ahhhhhhh: the booty
                 Of struck oil: the bonfires of struck tankers,
How alluring's that: not very. And yet all the time,
Waltzing, we waltz on the proud
And blissful pyramids—of a constant
        Present,
While all the time bombarding our atmosphere, licking up
The fear of media, of stars
    And—exploding cars. It's as if
The World ran without a turn, but wavered on its axis—till we
dive
Into the final polars of
The Universe. A place where the nature of things—cannot hide.
If only such a World were natural now!
If only there were no politic, no lie, no grimace, no economy
And all was done for all, and history
Was a continuous line.
But it is not, and each soul does itself induce
That imperfection of the World.
        For no soul is perfect—
We all have blabbed, blushed, angered ourselves and others
For gains.—But
            No one could've thought
Those little sins would come to this—to a World
Now overwrought with sin.

To a World rocked by the quibbling
                    Tribes within ourselves—which we hide—
And the reality and expense of War—of carnage. Which we do
not,
          But look upon with disgust, ending up looking
                    At ourselves, with distrust: for who are we?)

With body destitute
My blood distills—into the carpet vessel
    —Stitch in time—
    And thus, I culminate as time—I stand as evidence, of time—
Breaking, from the hem I knew—trespassing on
The quarantine of soul—a revenant keep to the bond—
                    The carpet vessel: made from rind and dirt.

Each bud—my bud—gives redress to the soil, the wet clutch of
the soil
          Shakes its limbs from brittleness—to nurse the mounted
budroot:
The soil is fertile of tombs, and all the ancient bodies—
To the present build and bind.
The soil is dug of tombs
                    They stock the concrete bearings farther lifting
To farther lift—the frivolous
          WORLD to fit the vitriol, withered towards
                    Its universal end of speech,
And further push the living buds to their own death.
On goes the revolution of the times—on goes each event
Happenings of small and monument.

I thus depart from who I was—
                    When I that old pursuant, of tangible Worlds—
I, the animate ghost who chased
    The minor spites and battles of the World;

I whose life so happily disappeared, whose history
Unfurled then furled again.

Death may find its way in wilderness.
                    It waits for human bone and blood
To blight and scatter all to dust—
                Death cannot kill of all us though.
Plenary planet this of capering personalities souls vapors
    Condensing together, never
Perished in full only
                Partly, growing back stronger-
-Sometimes weaker,
    Depending on the providential
Wag of HeavensCompany.

Death must spare the bushes—that do breed out
    Of our lives; and for man's faith and story—had they stood:

To give—resplendence—to our blood; to
                        Make—certificate of our strength.
Each tree a hardship faced, each vine sustained
                    By dirt tread on by the struggle
Of life. Each pink flower meets the light once after Struggle
before
Huddling in the vegetable darkness—that was
Each man's test of will his wins and losses. His sins and
All the greenery go;
That grew to form, from vegetablelife
Before death came—the scenery
That already fullspawned, that asserted solid roots do go—
Lifedelivered things, rootreared accomplishments, each one
goes
Into Time's fathomage unfading
            Into the sustaining dirt.

For what coursed rigid through the ground cannot, by death's dry
                Little fingers, little ones,
 Undo itself—and so it lingers.
I become—the woven dirt—
That lingers.

And so: the altered atoms of my blood—
Travel toward the pulse, the clock—
And transport through the progressing weave
That the death of men will forward sew—yet death in
Sluggish advancement of human, to human, through the coffinsnarl—
Into the carpet vessel; each potency—never reached,
Each glory day—never spun—
Will cast themselves into the dirt—and sew their lives into all time—
The constance of that fibered stream
   —slogs—with weight of men
And their wasted dreams—
                —undone by death—

(Death's pronouncement, the finish of power
     The final, forgotten season—mulled in defeat,
   Death—
     And his vagrant power seats
—Itself in old forgotten minds, so that
One finds
 A second life—that values
On the past.
And Value—cheapens the term, presented now,
When Age already robs the term—of lust.)

The boy's a

Salvaging of himself and his long tru
-ant dangling objects still
Dangling here downwards like testicles from
                    The crotch of an ancient
Past, plagiarizing the past
With the present, as like an dog would bite
                    Her ass everyday: and

And
—And the robbing of a sojourn present
By robbing the last age
   Piecemeal process fading
Term of lust and lust
And lust—
Is all men want—
   The Hedon of their prime are still astir—
Although the heart be dust.

   Life-laid-on-lust—most potent cusp—
Is all that burning in dying minds
            As OLD are stifled, and
   Their brim reality—
                Is left to yearn:
   Finding titles, for meager lives, o
      The idols of ambitious men:
            Invite the strain to future strength
                    We strive at length, for future gain—

         —Till fraught by the present chain
            Of Natures's reason.
                        She retaineth
The Holy Prize that
                Drive our endless work,
                Slowly churning through—fistless fight

For larger worth,
As press persuasive legions, of immortal time—
Upon mortal will.

And, time-by-watches will finish churning, one day—
When human want
Meets human end;
And when we die
The ancient tendons of the Earth—
Shall gain again their former ground
Littered from progressions of a needless race,
They will reclaim and seize
With emerald fingers—
Growing, to the ceiling—
And we shall feed those vines, that course untamed,
With the blocks, of our buildings.
Blocks—that once did feed the future of
The house of man.)

. ..   .

On the spang of pure metaphor, right,
A seed is in the ankle that flowers
From the shoulder of building. This makes sense,
And sense is what makes it from
Top to bottom of anatomy of poem—

—Exclude the rotating ganglia: blocks: houses:
Of thoughts that whirr paralyze the head
Like the slolom and
Solfeggio of begging birds—

—Or like the frequent signals of
Cachinnating machines—

And yet how are these
Like that? bird, machine. If one is to understand
That sonar goosing in the sick black that blips between
Two shades of two mutable links:
This correlation is barely made out from
The tornado. This intelligence
Is spangled with insensibility, one thinks …
You see what is to find is in the weald of mind
And in what is, the weald of mind
Usually not so linear, pluck the edelweiss
As firstly to expose to one the
Freaky notice of a relation
It ends up being a vicarious
Float for one who is to remain
Forever on the ground: muse as figures:
Useless epiphany: I wish all this were easy as giving money
To the poor. But any amount of money
—To the needy would be completely
Useless. I long for the death of this anxious evil: it is the mask
I place over my entire body. There is no other
Explanation than this.
Oh my. How the MEN of suffered silence holler
Like beaten dogs, alone and beaten spells
After the chance was lost for anyone
To hear it .^
Well I have earned nothing, earning nothing, but the long walk
Of questions, wrapped in tests
Which itself add up to questions
Never answered, never asked.
Never asked, never answered
As if the World—were Continental Drone
That plays The Game as does
Stone plays
Play a part in gravel roads

The unearned traveler—does break
The circles—he searched the circles he traveled
And opens bigger avenues—
And puts at stake, what—
—The former knew what Silver grew from this
Impractical search? To find
                    Some impregnable answer—from
A chance that such—had gone unsearched for years.

It is that fear of knowing
But one circle—it is that fear of rotting in
The bunkum that we stay in—and spend days in—
   It is that fear that—unknown altitudes
      Can populate—the
            Furthest peak
 And yet—to move through knowledge—
Makes those who do it farther from that peak—

So die the restless turnings of the head: while
The cautious face of logic tells
   What drives the scholar, or, what rule
                  Can Rule
         The current urbane Sense;
From this escapes a wind, not of convention—
   A further agent, made to charge the air—
Had orthodox not oer clogged—with detentions the
   One keen breath, the only one
Who begging asked, to shrug the bounds—
   —That made for all to see the ground, as
Ground—and only ground.

There lives by dregs a title meant to delve
   Beneath the even grass, that stands complacent
   On the lawn—

And count each ugly root each, unseen wrong.

. ..   .

In this precise WORLD
Beautifully precise,
There is a precise leaf—

—Upon a tree. It lingers on
The bough. The seasons
Scroll onward from
Temperate to Nordic.

Entire schools of other leaves
Break off, not spared
But one, all snapped
From sockets grown
Brittle at their ends.

The concept of diminishment that
Slinks in the cruise of the wind …
Down they go, on the waft of invisible
          Mechanisms, to clot the grain
—Of the dirt, forgotten yet never
Remembered in the first place …

One leaf remains
—Fastened—
To its bough, like a truant past its due
To fall, deciding instead
To stick it out in spite
—Of Everything

In this precise WORLD

          One sees that the
Precision is in
The mark of the whole
Thing, while the parts
In themselves are in want
          —Of discretion
There are irreverent
Anomalies in this,
Stillborn
Potencies that peel
Like dried skin.

(Perhaps the coital
          Paralysis is a hump
In the beating of time,
A mistake among the
Expanse of those solitary
Minutes gone without
Interruption

The leaf lives in a
          Pause, a sensory quiet,
Projecting the thing
Beyond the imagery
—Of shut planes

The metaphysical scraping
  Sound of one sort of time
Against another sort of time,
It is a grate on the nerves-
  -We perch, end to thin
End on the fencing between
Two oblivions. The argument
As to which hole is more

Livable and which reality
More feasibly able)

(The fencing too is itself
        Alive and in itself
    Contains the divorce of
        Of two other precepts
Not ever to be revealed
Although no doubt they
            Are indeed there—)

In this precise WORLD,
It is all dispersed into
            Jokes, frail jokes that clap
As thunder and then flit off
As Lightning, back into—
Nimbus that is
    Pusillanimous

Both dimensions are left ready to die,
    Yet like the leaf, they continue
        To exist on, despite the
        Laws of Nature, just as
            He may continue to
Thrust on, despite the
    Somewhat humorous
        Humoral blockage of—
Mythical serum to
    Conical Lingam

    MOLLOY saunters down
The road. He and his
    Bike are one and the
Same thing. Not fully

        Believing himself,
        He believes instead
    In the aging of the
        Foliage around him,
     Noting, somewhere
In the crevices that time is—
Endless manipulation

ARGUMENT: In this precise WORLD, a leaf hangs on a tree, past its due to fall; it is forever attached to the tree, thru the progression of SPRING to WINTER to SUMMER to FALL and again. Other leaves fall to the ground; this one leaf remains.

One sees that imperfections—anomalies—can sprout up anywhere, even in the crucial parts of nature—even if the entire whole of it remains perfected. This imperfection is caught, forever, in that duration of time in which its purpose as a leaf on a tree, attached to the tree, is retained. This pause verily is one sort of time between another sort of time; as in, both of these sorts exist, and are in conflict with one another—there is, first off, the time of the pause—when time pauses—and the rest of time that continues on, and on. So we see, the parts do not represent the whole, if there can be anomalous parts in an perfected whole. But which hole is more livable???? Which construct of time is the more feasible????? Perhaps this odd sort of pause is not an anomaly; perhaps, it is another way to look at things. We are on the fence about this; these two oblivions could hold two oblivions within. It is all a joke, really. Calling it a joke is the joke—the word has little to no meaning in this context, or maybe it does. I just don't know. I just don't know. The joke comes, fleetingly, as like the retraction of lightning, back into the sky, both oblivions—both dimensions— are left ready to die, and yet, exist on, despite the laws of nature—just as some poor fool may continue to relentlessly fuck a woman even when his foolish dick isn't even up. Both are contraries to nature!!!! MOLLOY proves all of this wrong—in the connection he deciphers, between himself and his bicycle. This is an image that seems to come out of nowhere … it is as useless as the word "joke" … or as useful, perhaps, regarding whatever context you may pick and/or choose for the benefit of this piece, this work, this pome—? Ha! We see, these two types of time are inextricably bound, not apart, just as MOLLOY and his bicycle are bound, and not apart. Tho, despite this discovery, we must continue to look at time as being nothing but endless manipulation, at least, in terms of the leaves on the trees, and, in how they change.

And yet, such thought can exist only fully in the crevices, and, so, is something not full at all, and is Anomaly.

(The names of reason
Change in their chime
With time, and the
Passing of seasons.

The relenting predicate
        Of dusk, too, in the days of lent,
Tells of Starvation

Of densest shade repealed
And pasted in the sky,
Betokening the real
   But wasted in the eye—
—An ultimatum of
Nocturnal AUTUMN.

But the padlock broken and
The hemorrhage of sunlight

Through gaps in the restraint,
Most conjugal bells for content, might as well
Be the jangle of manacles, a present chain
To produce a Hell of longing
        With a shock that is intestinal)

"ACKNOWLEDGEMENT: when in the debt of others
We pay the price for misdeeds
            By listening to them. So,
              Say your part in the debauchery
          The logy lipping
                Of dialogue
Making lives into strings
Of lives, in time

We do not know
In callowness,
To separate the chaff from the grain,
      Taking it all in as a single bad or
      Single good. Because of this,
Extremes are promptly
                Diluted.
The straining strings that bleak our
Magnanimous grin shade also the pulp
      —Of the sheen of our skin,
Folding attitudes of one into another
Everlasting silence, in time."

II. PERPLEXED COMIC MAKES A BET.

I have an eternity of heads
      Upon my shoulders—and I
Discard them,
      Like hairless plastic dolls, if I
      Lose one,
I conjure another
      From the basket of my insides.

Each bust I pocket has
      A sole pall and
      A single eye that
Haunt the sockets differently—

Depending on the bust,
      And in—the rifling of my busts
      I find—the kind of head—can greatly alter
Yet each one is the buttress for another.

And some are easier misplaced
      Than others,
I use the face and concepts
For an hour,
      And then I—trash the head
        —Like
A vapid dream—
—And swivel towards—a better chief—

   —To keep—my interior tribe on
The level—

I do not know where they
   Come from,
Why they exist,

   I fear the day
That they will disappear:

I am myself and I am someone else,
And both of these do linger in my lungs
Like tar. If I kill the other I kill,
I kill myself and the other
Lives more truly
Than myself. But not as full
—As both of us would
Be together full.

But I cannot kill the other.
He eats more and more into
Myself and more becomes myself
—With time. Meanwhile Myself becomes the other
That the other of before did kill
To be Myself.

We feed each other
—With ourselves. Speaking rhetorically,
If he were to snuff me
  Out, I would die and
He would live for me would
  Would make a hole where
   There was one, had

Always been—
I am the original of the selves the
     Embryo of sorts. I live like a skrit
Across the chill clime of space—

     And, he drips from embryo
     Of sorts, into his embodiment from
     —From the condensation of
          My sweat my tears
And dramas of the measly years.

HE is what I dream up o the
   Frailty of the embryo it
        Is misbegotten it is
             Moribund quite. It is
Needs that festering must
     Be had and
   The needs become
Another person lesser though and
Meanwhile reality is
Walled slowly in
By needlessness—

And whatever other person
     Or self the I dreams up remains
Stagnant in the burn
—Of what is tangible getting
        The ape desires, but
Not one touch beyond
   —The precipice of fantasy.

· ·· ·· · ·   · ··· · · · ·   ··   ·

I look happy on

The dry earnings—the drying prospects—of vain time—
That carried me so far—and wrung my wealth

As one wrings oranges, into juice—
And yet its taste at best is—doubt—but for the foreign drop
Of worn youth—

Though I am not the old anchor,
      I am not the Barnacle, I am not
The Perplexed Comic telling rotting
Parables—to bored
Children

And yet am angered
And sore. And filled with
The drink of dust. And I drink, drink without the tasting
All at once—as though
Life could be rejoined, without the tasting
      —Of this Dust …

            Realizing my insignificance
I gave up any path truly to
  Be taken by myself. And
Myself alone, instead,
Relying on the variable
            Element, to achieve stasis:

I appreciated the lack of control,
Centered behavior, circle to ellipsis

—That wavers—
  In other words peripherals
Would remain always blind,
      My low and hindsight, in that

Inner Eye …

(Yet that abyssal
  Guarantee, that pit of bull
Throws over—Inner Eye—
Another drape of clarity
        As permits a mortal of piss-and-vinegar
  Thought that is to be it the lesser
Contused upon arrival)

—Damned Epileptic Spar—the spine
And the ribs between that slams
With a frequency
Like gunning thunder …

(And come up to a supreme
    Fiction, myth nonetheless skewed,
        Gotten problematic.
          Skewed ball of crystal who
            Can lift it understood it
                As a mind unable to bust the shut
Clavicle of the door to the lavatory-
      -Without which my bones will fall
And I might as well with my pants pissed.)

. .. .

This day is less accurate
Than it has been before.

The bee is slowly starving
In the windowsill,
Thrusting furiously against the
Glass, masochism in desperation,

It is trapped in there.

Disappearances haunt
    These nervous commonalities
            Between the patents of creation,
Appearances now can
Only be simulated

A moth lies perished
On the carpet. Soon
The bee shall become
Like The Moth.

(Out
There there is
Commensurate moth swarm as
Big as WORLD commensurate
Humming of both eating
Eating, small maw
Together large teeth
—Teeth of Lepidoptera chewing
Holes holes in us

Holes, holes everywhere in us.

Many cloths by tears
I have darned them o the
Immense fabric of weeping
            Drying out in a crepuscular sun
Waiting in shame
—To produce cleansing
        For us all—

The moths they come

And they go leaving
Every pit gaping.
How was it all before: as

The pit of meaning you are then now is fastened to a stake—
Burning under the licking flames of another
Iconoclast.) Those relics I think of, of severe importance,
                    Are destroyed and
The lineage of the self
As indelible as the Greeks is
Made to destroy what it previously
                    Could only impede—

While the quivering ectoplasm
Of the soul, witnesses
The holocaust, damp in its innards—
Hungering for misfortune, for misfortune makes it hungry—
Reclining back, back, clockwork,
Ever the more comfortable,
So as to better observe the plagues of others, and this whilst
It is spared an attack upon its own tender system,
  Misfortune decides to strike a deal, that as long as
  One presumes to give a damn—

(I'll keep your eyes on the prize
Don't relish the pain says HE
Speak the pain down a bit
Corner it.)

Be meek,
Be suspicious, and
        Look for it before it
Finds you. You
        Want to be the

First one to find
            Out why you
Put yourself thru all
        This, and when, even,
    Since time or place are
    Clearly out of view, and,
        Well, I cannot formulate
    Much about it; can only
Live it with explanation-
                -Without forefront, without
Speaking then, I'll say what you
        All wish I wouldn't. And then
            The fault is on you, well,
                    Don't just stand there, understand,

That there are just and unjust
        Things and memories, and not
Only if you wish to destroy
            The carnal wishes that
Scribe across the walls
        Of the skull in elaborate
    Scansions: marvelous-
-Analyses of poetical
    Misanthropes that shut
        Their shaking selves up in
A prison,

            Only then, only then can
Can you promise death
To all the press, inside
        Yourself the whole time
And walking with a bum
Leg, you begin to beg, not
    By choice

But by occupation.

(Only now do you realize the scant ways of the ornery
Folk around you, that promise death, themselves, and yet
     Can only clearly state to me
That all just has to end someday
     (And then perhaps the log I keep
Will mean so much nothing, a pit-
          -To the WORLD I seek
     To destroy and replicate
In my own image)
My own image, keeping

Its eyes
On that nihilism, prize.) I
Wonder if am realizing
Previously existing flaws as mature physically
Or perhaps growing flawd with age, as though
     Buckling under the weight
Of consciousness: ahrmhm!:

"The WORLD is collapsible.
Humanity expands,
One day, will expand enough—

—When to the point, shall be knocking
Against—final barriers—of WORLD
Ballistics against the balustrade

I feel guts move and shift to different places
Within body, perhaps the methods of Beckett-GOD

Are haphazard."

....

III. PERSON MADE OUT OF EYES.

(HE cannot do so: do not beg him: and it makes him want,
Makes him want, to knock bully crown upon
                Upon the sledge of rock that contains him
Of rock that extracts the difficult strength found in a SPLIT soul
Leaving—just a man empty man. Fructified featureless
In sleeping stone—there is more personality in the rock
—Than the man. (He is a body that is
Within canker, though, displayed in this argot, an eternity.)
        And as for this asexual exchange it
Will backwards dissipate
Both body and rock back into carbon
        Just as with stone, he seethes
The rock has no prejudices. It takes
Everything in. The man
                Was just the first
To fall into the trap—because he was the weakest man—
                By using what little perspicacity has left
        In him that hasn't been drawn into the blank vortex
    Of the stone he hopes the rock will catch one day another
Another particle of another body shall that grow further
            The rock into a distended nonsense
But the man thinks it will free him. He does not realize the stone
Has the appropriate space to live many others despite that
someone
        Else has not SPLIT enough to be enticed by the innocuous
peace
        With which the rock presents itself. This exacting type of
Peace is prison. That it grows stronger by what it feeds on

—Is not to be disputed, though it becomes also
More chaotic, untranslatable, and ultimately horrifying
        In the cool acceptance of such paucity of worth
                And the stone and in him the intricacy
            Becomes a matter of volume
    Rather than substance. HOPE not that in stillness
            Would the object
    Be fully still, and stop:)

  See them. Know them. Stop.
        I see them and I know them but
            Do not know I see them
And only know them as
Vehicles for my own
        Righteous gain

This aging eye will die
After spending a day focusing
On something something
That it knows it sees and thus deplores.

        They pick apart me
Because they understand
—That I will only take
 Advantage of them
To claim the edelweiss
        At the top of the tooth
    —Of the pink fop of the Alps,

They fail at destroying me.
They spell out the answer, desperately
In vociferous rabble, trying to prove
Themselves enough to be respected
While still being seen,

        As like many men
Fighting over an amount of money.

This aging eye glazed
With rheum, is an eye that
Hears what the muscled magnitude of mind
—Blabs to it, and only that.

This eye looks upon them
        And hears nothing
        And sees much.

I saw the shine, only once
And waited it to thaw
For the brightness crystalline
And this dunce
In awe—

—The loam of the doubt this gloaming of the theories.

In my mind, there is a seldom case of brightness once realized
        Yet perceived, in coming from the encumbered bloom
            Of young logic, to be a criminal truancy,
A tumbling gaff down into digression,
—The loony dirges of a mind too weary in wishing.

Something fleeting as of glowing pendentives floundering
In the breeze, between fog—light meant to meander
Gone on and on and on
To the dull thack of the skull:

Fog is fog is fog is fog
    And what is not is something more than fog can channel
        Through its depths to be

Arrested fully by the blur
      One must be shapeless
        (In this progressing legion
           Of blind ruin … the environment blunting
       Syntheses that might have blended
         Eye with object. Any intimation of Rapture
    Is demurred by floating boats which calmly track
Some distance into sight with their motors
And subsume the docile elbowing of the fog somewhat
       In being prodigal images forms
     Disappearing and reappearing
There is little that is not
       Dynamic …
And in faith the FOG say

"Man stooped before confusions as apocalypse—
And pled to finish its design's
Far permit, could but Time not span
The route of man's muchcolumned mind—?

Live man's whole: marshal end: till its redemption,
And you could snatch the soul from a reflection
      And that my friend, is the demand

If the World were built as dust
At pyramid would be all things
(The human hill were brick and rust)

If only—muscle—taught the mind, and thoughts
Flew well on robust wings, and followed-

-Burly path
Cut clear in soil
Though what is mental

Never is to boil
Down to a universal scheme—that dumbly
Stocks what it can store.")

Weakness rivals all but namelessness.
It lives, is that what you mean,
As does a second Earth live
—With abrupt climate, always shifting,
        And deceiving
Always the glib.
It is a second store. Where bones can turn
To grain—its dusty floor
        At surge by hazard winds that treat
                These plains with human sin.
For Weakness rivals everyone
                On EARTH, at Plymouth
Only with a GOD who gave us

Nothing, but humanity and
        Silly Myths of
Greatness.

. ..   .

My faith is a subdivision
—Of two parts, it teaches me
The art of understanding that
Prayers crowd
His mind
And He hasn't the time—

—And the fear that answers may be
Nullified by prayers, for it
To happen—that this other GOD—

Of chance, will contract
Into smaller chance
When given the opportunity
     To slake the dried esophagi
—Of those, with water of the right
Polluted past the point of drink

Each diminutive person
Make prayers, and is it seldom
Answered if only they
          Did not say in their heads
                 That such should be answered
Immediately while the hands
Still tied together GOD does
Not like presumption, prefers to see the intellect
Revolve each question throughout many
Extravagant answers,
That flash innumerable round us-
                 -Till at blur,
          We wield our diminutive hands
From the top of a ladder,
     And grasp for truth and grasp
  For faithless colors—
   While what is right is not
By Light which burns—but
          Is groped for in the discomfort
Of darker standards. Where one knows not the place to fall, or
stand.

(Thick that follows along the ground
A liquid daunting swallows that
Which cannot be found

Cannot be found is only seen

Only after it is destroyed
This eulogy does not redeem
          This void)

· ··   ·· · ·   · ·· · · · ·   ··   ·

  Endangered ghost this man, this written man—
This man with eyes—the wane of milky moons
Lodged in the middle the pupils darkly centered
  In respective irises as afloat a nucleus confined
Within the Brown Irises; these two measures
—Of the self, encompassed
            By contemplative white
Bile, milky, bile, and, together, like a dark marble,

—Them bobbing on the surface of pale,
Some strand of sematic neon giggling in the hazel—
            As conjecture is what keeps the fact floating,
As all fact is premature, and his eyes are spherical ideas
That emerge—
From the must of the bile of the sclera

            (One rich in wanting a laugh
So strummed with the lilt of
                        Gentle sadness, as to appear
                  Likewise sobbing, choked,
                        Crest and fall, some tissue
  Of paranoid aspersions coughed
Out chuckling in blood)
        Beholding this shoddy WORLD flushed and tired WORLD
This ornate farce, gush of images, dreading a kind of cul-de-sac
                  With every assertion in the cornea—
As every assertion is a reflection mirrored—
        Each prone vessel seen, seems something

Created not by GOD but fiend who keeps
This man from knowing fully—what is to be known—
From feeling in his veins the flow of blood
        Although relenting a purpose to the sight
As one would, like you know

Would cartoon the Sistine Chapel: a purpose that the one who
Views it—mysterious hombre—takes to be the entire purpose—

(This laughter, loud, inhuman,
Pleases none—
But have I nothing left to give
That had before been given,

My soul is the blandest
—Of leitmotifs,
It is a grey soul of the mind
Look at it:
So much sadly riven
From what it was.)

On one of the many connections between the soul.^

… As sight cannot live, without, at least
A partly whimsical understanding of the
Things there are to see …

But in the tree that is blue and the ocean green
He names them such, enigmas blunted by names
The definition is sharpened with a wacky intimation
Derived from something not to make precedent
In words—but, perhaps, in words without form—
That buzz thru the trance of the thing that is witnessed
In the clouds congregate in the buildings and the hills

That each may stop being there, if not provided
With a constructive purpose for being there,
Of fear that all will vanish if not caught by the eye,
The images seem to resume when they are seen,
That when not observed will themselves, fluttering like pixies—
—Pursuing less visible designs, in the hopes of keeping alive
That which the trillion particles not solved by vision could only
Erect as spectacle, which shrinks the noticed scene
Into something less effectual than before,

There lingers a perception that would change what he ganders
—To be left with the idea rather than the object—
And though he may understand the idea,
The man loses the object. In vain struggling ends up
Unable to associate the once unspeakable notion with
What has become the now unspeakable vision …
The object roves far back, dwelling in a subterranean
Profundity, beneath the air … he moves thus backwards,
—Back apace back to where the object is again fathomed
                    And the wordless again is a premonitory clue
That, because it is not accessible, provokes anxiety
Like a gravitating horror that by lack of translation-

-Will capitulate to the pulls of future uncertainty
And hit his ground with an enervated plop,
He wonders, perhaps, if things die when they are not seen,
And when seen again are they different than before
                        And, when seen again
Are made the bogus bunk of dead conclusions
That plunge a knife into the wilderness:

. ..   .

Repetition breeds new meaning nonetheless from monotony
At first glance the WORLD has no
            Symbols where even intended, says HE:
Yet even where not intended there is vastness to pluck meaning
It is not necessarily mantra, because it is not religious or
therapeutic
Nothing more than limbo in this
                Derision that chokes and itself strangled

                The question expands like a perverse
balloon,
The balloon cannot be ruptured, or
        Deflate, because it is already doing that
It grows larger and larger, absorbing all meaning into a single
orb
    The balloon understands meaning only as indivisible,
This in turn results in an exclusion of meaning-
    -Which brings us back to monotony, the inverted circle

All it boils down to blood of lamb, the sacrifice of velocity
For the sake of a meaning turning ever into something else
Since if not permitted to move, will move within—
        Since movement is found in that which does not move—
The result after aeons of the twin temperaments of conflicting
poles,
Which, when juxtaposed, apprehend the unity of all things
In being the cellophane of this obesity, this balloon,
In being the balloon itself,
            In being a cache for the sums, rather than the sums,
        The sums are different each yet and have respective
opposites
This causes the question to turn ever into something else
An overwhelming period of exhaustive research
—Perfectly good insanity. A rock got faster and

Faster. And then stopped. A cradle for the fossil
In which you are stuck. Say HE:

"Fair trade."

. . . . . . :

IV. A PLACE THAT IS COMMON.

In the street, there are two
Visions … projections. One is—
The streetlight and also there is
A man below the streetlight waiting
For the pause in himself—to foil—
And—him—to be on the way
—And the ground below him to
Disappear the streetlight
Is a secondary object. It illuminates
The primary object the man is the
Primary object his circulatory system
Still is throbbing—he, still living, you see,
Much as one can, as such merely is contained
Within the scene the streetlight,
Proving the value it has in exposing
The connivance of little moments
Little moments together into
Big SOMETHINGS subliminal
Sublimities as regards the brief
Canvas on which painted is the moment-
-Described heretofore, and many
Others that fix themselves
In the place of an instant

Simple screws the screw simplicity in.

The streetlight seems a flaw within the flow,
                    Its strange and quiet service
We shall never know
—What the something is, he waits
For it—in a manner near inanimate—we shall
                        Walk past the dude, slightly
Agitated in the gyre of our abstract,

Our own abstract pursuit towards
Distractions shackled to in our
  Pocket, the crumpled dates,
Schedules that rouse our
Crumpled minutes with
A turn from sedation—perhaps exchange

A neutral glance with the
Man, and then continue,
On our way, (having by now
Following the seconds' exposure

To that apparition forgotten or,
At least, put out
Out of mind why the man happened
        Man happened to be
In that position—)

—And later, we shall fall asleep and
        Dream obsessively
In foggy fragments, about streetlights,
Awaken previously, perplexed,
Only to wake up again:—

(I have so countered every sun in memory
With moons as fake and guileless at the nucleus

    The loft complexion paces blush to blush
  But all of sky hangs same
Above the populace.

        A Diamond may be rough with loveliness
  As illness may inoculate with spores,
          Ecstasy—rows the surf, and woefulness
Is laden there, in there, the surf—

—Depression keeps a Door
To open Bliss.
But so—the realism of this our Strata
Is that it borrows nothing is no twig
To roots—that burrow deep
To someplace nowhere
But is invented, like a miracle,
Out of the paranormal air,
—An air we cannot breathe.

These polar passions of a Haw a Cry to us
Not are in twine, by the—same soul—

(NOTA: a laughter shared between two folks
Was what I heard and could not
                Understand,
It spanned awhile between the two
And plummeted like their eyes
From one another, like a
Shortly shifting pawn—
To—message—a connection hovering
    Between
—The queen and king—like
A bleated pop of cinder
From a fire—like

A sting or welt that popped as well
        —With the right prod.

And so I dig the dearth of what had been
My composite of what a human does,
And
I cannot find a reason for the buzz
Between the two,
The momentary comedy they had seasoned
With momentary snickers seems illusive,

Gems that flicker flimsy
Sources of some secrecy tween
Bipeds one another and
        —The barely visible forces—and
I do not know the gems
        That make the forces.)

These polar passions of a Haw a Cry to us
                    Not are in twine,
        By the—same soul—

But things so opposite, it is perceived,
Should have own spoon and their own bowl.
This hummed duality of folk and feeling,
The toils of the system and our system are
All same capital for banks of mood
But different in their getting and their rhythm
And different in their ending and their cue.
The vote still lives—our minds eat separate slices—

Few people wish to think at all on dreamed conjectures that
Purse the limits of mankind together,

Because the Strata will not give them license.
They'd rather not go linking sun to moon
But moons may be like suns for what both give—
—That bridle churned confections of the sky
And liken the aural plane above
Into a single stain—that lives
For hours, till things coalesce,
And the single Color dies.

Ironic: they would swagger for
A single color—to Define their WORLD. And
          Really all that they are searching
For—is power—in a brick of verity—
—That may they
Swallow, to abet their souls,
          Which swell like carbonate questions, in a sea.
Sadness, I think, holds some impatient ghoul
Of happiness, as placidness does hold
A type of anger anchored in the quiet
That is, not yet, entirely entertained—and
          So releases from the brain in silence,
Floating over the sentiment
We recognize
     And darkening that hue of amity
With a tang of solipsistic fury
  That presses on the photo
     Of our eyes. Says HE

"In solitary rooms
The light does ease the ignorant
With sure continuum—
He sees his form to end in skin
His eyes find sustenance
In reading not the Skeletons-

    -Which in a pause of light,
Would throttle the mind's
New weight and agitate
        Each deadened sense—
And give dimensions, and give depth, to his perceptions, of his
skin."

. .. .

It grows within the buildings I remember.

It tolls the busy thugs in alleyways.
A sound that mutters from the waterlights
(Kept shining, through the shadows of the bay)

And all the embers broken on the pave
Fall dusty from the soles of broken men: whose
Small light barely buffed the traffic lanes—
—Then feeling something—overtake—they ran.

It sleeps within the city I remember.

Of those who drown their coals, in cityleagues,
Some liquid shadow—shying from the flophouse
—And, of depth—as they close in on their dreams

The petty stream of—little confiscates—
Of levels up, but levels from the goal …
It lends, for sake of spirit—little seams
—To sew, all egos torn—but only sews …

The few, whose eyes have met their visions, toast
To empires pits above the rheum—
It cannot touch those men—so spends the doom

—On bitter barflies bitten by their banes.

It rains within the rooms. I remember.

. ..   .

(The shoes I wear,
Eke out their soles,
Slowly, with leather patience …
The heels and toes of them are thinning each.

Moving up the fabric isolation of the
Suit, are selfless pants moody
With starch and
Softener—
There are minor pinstripes blazing
Their minor trail down
The wilderness of the weave of the
The
Suit
   The
Ubiquitous garb, of city business
The
Reticent dichomedy of the polyester
          Cosmopolitician.

I shower using the last resin
Of the water tower at the top
       Of our building the kindling
Of the day already seared
Past cinder into
Tranquil pleasant ashen pieces, as
I wake up—the attitude and ache of the day releases—
Maybe it's the altitude. And—

—More so, every minute,
—I feel myself—thinning—like my shoes—

Look at yourself, look in the mirror, you:

The dotted mammal of my tie lying beached
And sodden upon the
Buttoned cotton Oxford cloth
Collared shirt with
Sleeves,
Braying for its life, like a boring whale
            On sand

And the tailortuft
        —Of my shirt, and
The Windsorclot
        Of my tie could
      Choke:)

Informant taking off tie feels
        Sense of freedom from the noose. He is sketchd
In oblong and imperfect
            Composition. He is
   Beautiful and his arteries
Walld in by cholesterol:

A long day, fuck it, and a long
Time coming, this long
Day—the elegant ease in passing
Of this week was rhetorical
Fiction—

Fiction the snickering wire of this week is

—An extension of scales: ophidian poison, slow,
   Slow, inflates the glands and
Has come, after teeth sinking
To a Friday that chunks
   All errant errors into Errata
—So, after much long
          Skedaddle from awareness …
And with fatal puncture … the venom
Runs its course and suddenly
Popped out of nowhere,
Reminding one—
—Of dreams in the ruin collected
Collected in an absurd Rolodex
—Within the brain. I kept stepping
Kept stepping stepping
Barefoot, through the lithic stale
Of this critical mind upon the brambles
          Of my own Disquiet—the static matter
Of the figurative—halting before
And after also every
Word spoken, as though
   Snared in hesitance as to
             What I had, exactly, in mind
          To say—thinking perhaps
   That perhaps what I had
   In mind to say, would further chintz these,
These Moralities hung like stilted honors
Across the puny pigeon of my chest,
And instead something I say, quite different
Quite different—

—A colloquial mutation of inner
Quibbles: hah: lighted just a bit by the
   Brief drone of an accurate thought—

A heavenly thought, and a long time,
 A long time we had of it made a day
—Of it thinking mutely sometimes with our
Eyes and coffee quickly the parturition of
Spoiled beans, becoming lukewarm like this thin

Spiel: that is, our lives: it would seem to philosophers,

    That as much as we stay
Here sitting, crossleggd
And with lagging time
Doze, much as
            Well waken in forty
Billion decimals of scatterd
    Rock cruising up the pathic
Decibel and chiming the way
Through modular canto
Aiding with hearing aid
The fail, volume of ailing
            Ears—carving out a spot on
The couch for his fragments
 To collect and spin together
Delightfully musically
Each time we break
            Into pieces we even see the
        Least part of ourselves
Glog the air with
        Particles participating in a flurry
Of Great Things to be had
By us, before being had
        By time—but when Senility
Becomes static when dementia
        Lacerates a dying head,
I will lead my sleeping

Particles to bed, with the
Highest decibel in hands
Fizzled by rheumatism they
 Shake as I collect the powder
—Of myself and listen
To the musical strains of
Work of GOD, and delve
The gulf running deep in
          The ecstasy of songs
       This is reportd at the climate
Of Blues there is clarity
Clarity in the tuning
   To the lark of a wrong key, the cant
Of many greats
Flicker the fates
Of him then fade into
  Lesser glories pouring
Out of dust

Says HE: this is what is inside a thing:

Fogginess. Sun and moon. Art is the math of self and self is
The artistry of GOD, not fully done
But close. Art is comfort. It allows us to prove the soul
          —As something deducible. We create the myth
And name it such and such—
It always meant to presuppose
       Itself with the dedication
—Of a lie. This falsehood is our
Greatest asset—one finds hope
            In what one snatches from the
Experiment of his own thin air
—The calculations of this intangible spirit,

Tweaking a node of chalk feverishly against a surface
   Attempting reason but without the reason
Which means we must start—

(From the concentrated origins
Of our speechless experience
As to what reason really is.)

Hm! We have not fully collaborated
—As a species. The mind is a flame of ice.
These spectra of motives stem invariably
From vice, or bleed without notice
From the canthus of our eyes
These things are not fully thawed,
  And the flame refuses to still its jerk.

We are miscellaneous seraphs without fledge
Yet flying far by the internal action of the self.

I suppose HE meant for us to be
Continuous greenhorns. We are
—Until some chance fatality, suffering
From the trauma of birth, we have a delirious,
Delirious homesickness for those minutes
Before consciousness

We are perpetual tourists, visiting HIS creation
    For a bit: then back to where
We came from, eager to return to the fecal nothing of the dirt-
-And feel the familiar worm feasting on our curse:
Growing fat off the dead flesh while we
Do not grow at all:

Beckett-GOD met me at the streetlights, and when I woke up

said that

He sees the thing and knows its opposite.
It is a kind of argument
                —Against the significance of it. Inevitably,
He must approach the thing twice,
Once as an image without purpose and again
          As a purpose gone blind
—Of its vessel: so that the assertion of what
                It is, suddenly holds no credence
              And becomes absurd:
   He decides, then, to falsify an exponent, which he will
Convince himself is in the thing … an exponent that can be
Understood, and inevitably due to the polarity of men-
-As regards what can and what they cannot understand
He believes a strong contrary, to have suddenly taken
precedent
Over the original meaning battling
        For the negation
              Of it to be expressed
From within some strange metaphysical
                  Chamber of discontinuous void
        The result of all this being only an obstinate unseen
            —In this simple blue vase. By this token,
                Inevitably, the conclusion is made
That the kernel of the thing,
If gotten easy, could be as lost with the same ease
          To us, it is challenged always by its contrary
For not this picture of the blue vase moves us
It is the understanding of a clear motive for the picture—
It is the fierce promulgate of idea, given a vessel,
It is sure dictum found behind the painted physic
                That moves us.

. ..   .

        SAKES ALIVE! ... well,,,
Each man presumes to be
        A giant but a giant only
To himself. He tells others this ... while they believe
That he thinks such be true
                Their own personal assertions of themselves
As giants, to repudiate the HELL they are to come upon—
This keeps others from seeing the giant
                That is in him. So they placate him.
        The gestures of their faces askance
By the tulle of flattery
That in feigning insults his
Big talk—which in to them are definitions malleable
And to them, he is harassed by the present cangue of his
thoughts
                From which the head of thoughts is
pullulated
Out of the restraint, is born out of doomed rebellion to the
restraint
Until he escapes, but escapes only with half of the idea
And then, like a slave recently
Freed feels the
Embarrassment of hesitance
As regards his truncated emancipation
It is a monster exclusive to him chides against the zealotry
—Of his circulate theism
Makes him question the myth he shall report
                But the uncertainty of his principles
                        To others does not shake the ground
As does it to ground beneath his stance
The heat of him to others is benign
And in this heat is rapt the sense
Of a portent he shall not stake in speaking

For fear the massive shrink of his domain

Into a mortal passive he would repugn
In a volley of prose
          Because the breadth of domain is untranslatable
          Whether it be domain of idiot or of genius
He gives himself to the idea of the idea
Rather than weaning it from what it is, by the grand folly of
words
Hoping to keep the denigration of design
To a minimum

     Before the overreach of bellied resonance
               Purports to cause the planets to align
     And to this end he carries out the impossible
               Only as much as could be carried out,
          And then, in understanding of the limits
                    The quarantine of mind in an extravagant room
     Relinquishes in him the pabulum of half schizophrenic-

               -And half prophet, making him a child old,
Who is old in effort, rather than age, and
          Thus: regrets the kenosis of his affect:
For the sake of lighting up the havoc
Only for others to know it as something
          Half explained

And from that comes the next conclusion—
(One first senses the errors in the source of the thing
          That if it were truly perfect, would represent
What it was and only what it was, without becoming host
To some paradoxical suspect with which it feuds invisibly—)
And yet, to call it FEUD would make caricature
Out of that which is neutral

Being that the thing exists, and does only that,
It cannot possess the feeling of itself nor any sense at all
Much less rivalry towards the dissenting particles present in it
   The thing does not care, and does not wish to care—
Such an impassioned agon, we that find in these inanimate
objects
Would certainly—by the fervor we know is of such
consciousness—cause to split
   The objects down to atom, and the atom
Could divide only, and divide that weird and ultimate
Pragmatism that deigns over nature:
The uniform neutral blah given to all reality would split to a pair
   —Of senseless things that of them neither contain
The opposite, nor the frank meaning
Behind what they are being,

Which proves the ghost of this duality I shall describe it
As a choral piece that might occur like irony in the spiritual
Bulk of this cathedral this mingling the basset
—Inherences with strange falsettos nether accents of itself

Allofit is invented by the value
Of our own cloven imagos of the WORLD,
And so, you see, it is to personify robs all matter of its power,
   Because a person is, to put it bluntly, not an object at
all
We do not hold the power of something that stays, and never
leaves,
   As Borges would remark about his keys
  While the WORLD of seen total of actual as known,
Need not evolve to continue to exist
It need not swerve, nor alter, nor gainsay the influences of the
past
   It knows no past nor future nor present

It is the birthright of the infinite.

(The power of the disaffected hauls tangible forms away
From this cancer of duality, although to us the lichens of the
answer
Thrive in feeblest mist.)

One comes, again, to the conclusion
That no idea can be only what it is
Without mutation to the counterfeit,
Without initiating a thrombus
In the collective brain of man—

An idea must be born from the mist most
Feeble thus would have the power to swerve
From the origins of inspirations on which it were based
Or else become, as I have said, the counterfeit—
The inverse is true for solid things,
Which can and will be only what they are
Unless man make a meaning of it that is myth
—And myth must drain the power from the thing
By representing the figurative rattling of our heads
By making oblique that which is not oblique

The joke that GOD has played on all of man:

The maelstrom caused by contradiction
Simply such a thing is artless yet deliberate
—And all of MANKIND must never know
How it is deliberate
Or how deliberate

Duality is the flaw of all creation. By appeasing
Ways of the dominant perversion of the WORLD

By relenting to contradiction—duality—by making such a thing
Into art, we have, instead, brought the universe contrived,
By giving it a purpose we gleefully understand
		But understand, only by shrouding it—this in turn
Begets no such shroud in the judgments of men but a false
fathoming
That in the recognizance of the universe as equivocal
Denies the true reasons for the thing, which indeed are not
	Equivocal—indeed, they are quite obvious to GOD
The great turning of polemic upon the head, with generation
And generation next, is nothing more than a blocking agent
Leading us away from an answer
That, in the first place, simply could not
		Be ever known ever and to give respect to this fact
By dissolving our core theories into antithetical vague—
It will cause us to stamp a different name on the thing,
unconsciously,
And this compulsion to fabricate an
Answer is closer to what GOD had in mind
Except for the fact, the thing already has a name, a name not
told us
That cannot be told us, not because it is beyond our
understanding
As is the accepted view of most, but because
		It is a thing that can be something else, and, more
than that
This vacillation is to whatever GOD
There is the meaning of what the object is
And from this, we can but understand that this blue vase
Holds no truth but in the destruction of what it could be
			Destruction caused by the
Foolishly immediate appraisal of what it could be
			Which, in turn, results in the destruction of The Idea
...

We lift one tessera from the mosaic of things
And call it different. By removing the tessera we remove
The mosaic, and think it not so big a deal ...
                We must not even try to name ourselves
As people, without bleeding generalities. We must not name this vase
Or else risk what already are, the heavy warp of
                The Idea, into An Idea

—An Idea that tho deficient, nonetheless is
Necessary, for order in the development
To properly catechize the thoughts of previous men
Which is a need infects the present men,
I feel perhaps that one before the first was only right
And nothing more than TRUTH has followed after,
And what power is seen again is myth
And only myth that one day, comes alive,
And when this happens GOD shall not exist. Humanity—
Shall become the GOD forged
  From the slow believing of our lies

(Something very wrong
In the smulch of the sun
        Something wicked in those
Acrylic hills, painted green,
Only ooze attempted green ooze
—On which to base the gnarl of his imagination
And the sky a paltry blue—?
Marks from the Green hands,
        By a CHILD whose marks
Are still to be made: this portrait of a land jut deep
Into the puissant opalescence
—Of chattering mystics that live
In his stomach, their magic is

    Badly transferred, they wait, disturbed,
As he grows old, to be dismissed)

....

V. THE CASE OF DIABOLICAL.

There is the fear the winding still
        That undulates for twenty years, between
Buildings. They are of brick, which have cropped the strings of what
                        They are, into a tangential answer
Rather than a question that exists, as such the buildings would negate
Themselves. If this were to happen negate
Everything for the sake of being what they are now
Which is not much. This building in particular is an eye
        That observes the city with disinterested fatness.

        All is not lost, just partly lost
Only in what was gained could not
Speak the misery of its becoming
Could only
Work as an inference: the insensitiveness of being
Without birth—go forth then
And tell the tale of the structure. Tell us
—Of its blatant history. But the finale will be an utter like no edge
        That before the axis could rock it down will fall
upwards
Simply in the axis need not to be tenuous
In order for the fall to include itself,
It must use this ability to waver, to form a negation
                        And thus it will fall upwards

We know the news already spread
The news is already told. We need no galloping Paul Revere for
us
But therein still the absence causing fear
As to what could have been extant if the building had decided
To sway to fall downward rather, as a result of the sway
What could have been is thus illuminated in the imagination
        And in the sudden purgation of the meaning, one rises
And enters a room at the top of the hunk of the structure—

One finds in the room the oldish magnate at his desk
Scratching out the fiddles of his clasp
And wishing for something less fated
To succeed down to, the atom purity
Of fact:

(Vampirism
In extremis.

Drawling delegation
Of a point with which
        All agree already merely
  Massaging own throats,
Happily under the yoke
        Of rigid partnership

These friends of the firm …
        They do not bother
With your partake in nastier
Contrivances, perfidious retardant
Of alcohol, sensitive proclivities
Leading depressant but no mess
Come to light, only

The sycophantic publican,
Crouching in a corner
—Of the room,
Foaming at the mouth as he
     Is asked to approach his prize,
Gathering no other evidence
          To prove his own greatness
     Besides the absurdity
              Of shuttling papers—)

Mistake of the fallen,
He has fallen.

And the long journey long from
          From pole to pole
     Exacerbates the tragic flaw
   Exacerbates the catharsis
It all depends on the destination, and when it will be reached
               It all depends
          On the translation.
               He has fallen and deceit is in the smoking of fruit
               —Smoke rises in curlicue syllogisms not rising
Without certain entitlements
          And the next despoil of boom
               Plangent in the denouement
When vulnerabilities are coiled back
Back, after the story is done, into the pliant soothe—

Gone are the fraggable accoutrements
Of people and their lives:
Like a painting devoid of humanity.

(He is not the purpose of his movements.
He is neither the manipulated chord cathedral heft

       Driven out the brass phallus
Cracking the ears of constituents of GOD
Nor is he disaffected, stupid, boringly pompous
This mastery of the rim
       Compels us to think of him
     As the traversing of sobriquet
  Hoping for tourniquet itinerant pneuma)

What it is is this: between what we know
      And what not to know
Or how to know it
Without eventually
   Precluding genesis
And then left with what is left then
The name his name
Has the scent of obloquy
It is in the squirrelly fingers
Of his peppered mustache:
It is in the condensed power
Of his neutral stare,
Smoking to the butt,
Beckett-GOD: The exile of
Silhouette from
Face out of profile each
  Semantic detail of
Wrinkle in feature importunate
  Style head
Shunned hair
And what
Little follicles white turning
    The lamp upon your
   Clustered atoms assembled
With long long passage of
Time into something unfortunate I turn

My lamp upon you you

You old brittle relisher of cultured
Coquetry towards cuckolds at
Their expense

This cult mulling
Whether pariah or
Or merely sole prancing
Jeremiad and never again tested
Tempest, rogue being,
Squeeze juice from the folds
Over carcass

I judge with
With light upon your face,

I find why exactly
You meant to be

(Me, I would chronicle
Myself maybe to
Plumb answers, out

Of words, but words cannot be answers. They are flat
Things they are curved objects on a page,
Illusory records of hours remembered, being
Meaningful or useless ones. But what can words do to help a
dying man?)

. ..   .

… Cheap excuses. Ego death.
The day creeps on

Each breath is counted
Each sigh is extinguished
Nothing poignant is there
    —Sarcasm and doubt
    Is there—

Whatever life I manage to
Build—will spend in worry
            Of destroying it, due to
            Mortal limits—tread lightly,
Or try to—when it comes
To things like this

No euphemism for
Me, I think I was
Born a question,
Something songed
        In whispers rushing
Meaning summoned
Solid to the surface
        And bleeding

I have not much to
    Live for besides these
Untidy and illegible
 Things that are
Confusing I am
Dismissive of them

    Alternative materials move
Carefully between hands,
    The gristles of my best end
    Up being unnecessary
As the pen that needed

                    To bring them to life
—Why then, should I bring them
To life questionmark

Write because need
 To. What to write
Then, without a
Subject on the mind?
Am left to describe
The lack of subject—
—Just write just let
Words develop the
Stilted WORLD emerging
After eons out the chasm
                    To chase the
Farthest lengths
Where I can see all
And know most after
Centuries of some fake thing,
                    An obtuse experimentation, sincere
                    Though penultimate innovations—
                                Germination of an
                    Idea too quick
            To be realized, there is a quiet
I have known, a strange
 Manner of sound shaking
The ground

Let the past fully ready
Itself for my obsessive
Calculations, I must know
Once and for all what
I did right, and what
Wrong, the middle ground

Between these two visions—
What truly scares me is this

They say, must be
The magic of—
Some mad frink, lost in the head
Severing levitations—would have got me
To it—before they reach the sublime
                    Something is muffled
The more I think of—
It the more it flies
Away from me tragic
 Assimilation of individual
Mind into the dim wit of
A box lightless

I know longer than
Most, and less than
The lot. Perhaps my
Standards have risen,
If so—
Good.

Literature casts a long
        Shadow, influence
Usurps willful creation
But the spirit is still
    There I hope it is still
            There—

            In these words, meanings
                Come and go, switch character
                Upon a band, roll over onto the
            Opposing belly of themselves,

These words have the
Courage to be wrong—
        Compels our odds to favor
An eventual correct result
    Impelled to the back of bad
        Humor and to the front of a—
        Lucky streak, give me the
Quick correction, so that
        I am able to expand upon what you
        Already know, exclaiming that it is
My own, and stretching the
        The meaning thin, hissing out
The compression of the meaning
With my own parlance of grief
—That numbs the meaning, slightly,
    I will make arduous
The simplest
    Of tasks that in slowness would percolate
The slow, stupid grounds of Emotion thru the filter of—
Experience,
    The confusion
Is related to waiting for the fall
Into my empty lap—belated
Princing moment, giving me
Walk without stumble

        Like rainwater in pan
    I watch my measurable
        Life measure upwards slowly
And eventually, with lack
    Of care, brimming life over
The top spilling tears
    Droplet tears the logic
—Of—lilylivered mind

Is of one kind—
A single crow marching
Across the pavement of
A vacant road

I will answer only if
The question remains
Squawking the dearth
Of another fool. I resist
Ranted falsities and
Hobnob theorizing and
Place those batty eaters
In storage to eat themselves
In misery

The question is cured
In one second, without
My help, and what
Does one do? Gape at
The answer and wonder
How such creatures
Could walk and with each
Step planted new crops of—
Faith, raw and hungry
With want of contact,
Follow fallow words of the teeth,
Mate with the meaning to produce
A new hybrid of meaning wholly
—New so so yet so so we blame
Blame our previous follies on
All the facts, which are unmade
Because of that modern emotion, made ageless

…

A spark that weasels out of

precarious
    Situations, had done hard in the heart
            In the hazard of all this
        I know that GOD shed,
        Shed his skin into the
Dough of this idea

(It is the adjacent to
 JESUS and in vivid
Wreckage suddenly
        It remains after the
Kiss of Nazareth
Pompous thicket of—
 Thinking drinking
Too much not enough
It seems to forget ha ha)

Do not fear
Nothingness, it is
All we ever had and
All we shall see is an
Everything shagged
Of life, although it is
There cannot be
Touched

Life is not so bad
    It is bad sometimes
Other times it is not
 Bad most times is
Bad bitten by the asp
Of bleak history,
I seek to change
All that, the light
 Is naked

The spirit is
    Gone. Dejection
Pursues me like
    A piranha stuck
    In blood—I have no
    Exit strategy how can
      I become able to beat these
These snares?

Nothing to probe
    But to myself prove
An edge on death,
        Who inches inch
    By inch, approximating
    My demise

Free the living from
Death, free the dead
        From their lives,
      History is now shut
          Down—there is nothing
Left to describe besides
Some dust that has been
 Coughed up out of a throat
Attempting to vocalize
An explanation

        Living in mist. Cannot
See end. An everlasting dream that quakes
        This prete,ntious confessional
And is made up of many bands
Bands of light bands of dark
            Voices crowd the realm with

Paraphrases. This realm this
Everlasting dream, within waking
But not so much that the eyes still remain halfopen
         And halfproverbial I choose wisely
The next move and hope no danger
      Will come of it tired of being
Tired of life I cannot-
 -Write the quandary of the
Creative spirit it is
Answered halfway

Everything is gone
Nothing is here
I have a life that I do not
 Know about and it is there
Lurking for better or worse
As such I am very quiet

I …
Anyway my next thought
Is this one:

(The marasmus of spirit
Crest and fall just write
 It doesn't matter what
 Comes out just keep
Doing it my heart is in pain) must be something there
Rising out of chest, perhaps a hint at something
To be understood as
Transcendence I neglect
To cherish what is
Inimitable what is the
Feeling like what must one
Do, to become words,

Feel them shift like
        Minnows trapped in water that
Collects in desultory pockets around
        The arroyo of the definition
Or, rather, it is like how
A fetus would kick to be
Freed from its quarters—?

    —What is that feeling like?
What must one do? To
    Become the words????
            Feel them shift, alive,
        Under your skin,
Little cells roaming like
        Like misfits in the
Fog, waiting, waiting to be
Understood

Speak not ill of
Those who are
It in the head

Just write just

Cleansing system constant
Garbling never stop
Work not effort not
Proud enough for that

Piecemeal from icons—
        Loath to find any
Rogue wellsprings of
Forgettable evolution,
Ever so turning slightly

Fallow the same ingredients,
        This recipe for success
Turning fallow

        Am not thinking about
What am writing only writing it, to see what
Signals softly gather momentary
Momentum on a loose circuit: random
        Rhythm arranged on blots

Roll me towards EVEREST
Roll me up the hill please GOD.
        Bring me back to control

Symmetry gone septic
Gross litany disentangled
And shooting, like a nova. The
                Pestilence wrought
Fragments, lies bare in
Forms

There are things which
I shall never understand,
Well as things I will
 Understand too soon for
The meaning to fully be
                Revealed to me. The worst
        Part is that, I know this will
    Happen and can
Do nothing
About it

Metaphor:
There is an endless

Machine of hob and nail and
 Knobs, and tails perpetually
In a movement of secrecy
To the outward eye, there is—
One sort of dynamic,
 Deeper in, yet unseen is—
The panic of movement
That bleeds
Into lessness

(More times I have tried
To make claims of truth
Than truth there was to
Sequence in kind verse.)
                And, found that the inherent
                Chapters of our thought are
 Hardest to thumb through—
 In that, what comes naturally
 To us, whatever cognizance
It is—if attempted to transform
            From head to page will seem as
Though one were perpetuating
   Nothing at all, for what are we
 As we see ourselves but great
Nothings, ghosts, that walk and breathe,
So complex is this idea of—
            Accuracy in the delineations
                Between the verve and toil of—
                Our minds and this long, prostrate body of meaning,
                    Scribblings of a flaccid remnant …
Our minds, which are the makeup
—Of who we are, and yet
Who we are is seldom seen
   In words without seeming alien or not quite right, and when

It is right—yields not to any
Analysis whatsoever as to appear
                    Appear illegitimate anyway,
        Thus, my writing is a constant cycle
—Of negation, where things
        Said wrongly to others seem right
To the one who said them and
                    Things that are rightly said
            Seem with merit to everyone
But the one who said them.—
            The MOON is late tonight.
    A spell is over the water
And the air. An essence
—Of corporeal solemnity
        That drags out gnats and
The flies to eat the calm away
Much as my ankles—
Futility is cast like a die,
A token of chance that
Expires
Before it can be redeemed, so that the gesture in itself,
                    Was worthless when flung—
So, hope only nipped at the
Corners of wanting, enough to cause
Salivation, and as soon as it was
 Snatched dissolved

I had another MOON in mind—
Besides the one I have described.

Flatness betrays the dimensions
Of this WORLD perhaps
Tho it is merely a flat darkness,
Perhaps forms will take shape in my

Eyes when the light of the MOON
Flicks on from off:

(And that nameless, Speechless Light—turns on—
By cruel favors—
    That, gag up, open, despise;
By spurious deals settled on
Mordant tones and balking—eyes.

The speechless light sustains
Through bits—of—odium—of
Past fights. Fingers
Upon wary shoulders that blacken

—To empower fucking spite.
The light—is growing colder;
The air is bitter
With the talk of soldiers.

But what makes
Speechless Light from this? Only that
The speechless risk—of acting or reacting
        Back
      To
Other evil's subtle hate—
—Keeps peace within the savage light—

Keeps the dim and savage light,
From being any badder lit
Although—its light is bad enough, as is.)

．．．．．．．

VI THE EDITING PROCESS.

(Compels raw sun to rise—and bear the hoard
They—cling—they race—from comment to request:
        Those human colors—each life—seems separate lord—

                That to the yellow edge—they do ignore
His healthy reign upon the east and west—
            Attests each man a title—though the core—

—Of heaven rests—yet holds EARTH in his store,
                    Next to the stars—beside official planets—
And unofficial ones—that men look for—

—But cannot find—the
Spatial remnants, storm-
            -Where men can hear
But cannot see far past.
—Solar units—man's one unlocked door—

So we beat our chest, and name our force—
As better than the SUN—or all the rest—)

Ennui. It is necessary that
We find something
To do—that in doing
We create,

We create,
While wrist to wrist
By the shackles
Of Inertia

Boredom expands the
Question until the

Absence of an answer may
Be nothing but a trifle
Left unfinished

We slam like steel the perpetual
Nagging inspiration
Upon a rock, hoping
To cause fire:

(Blindness. Cold and
            Dark. Malignant
Delta of sorts arriving at the
The cleansing point of
Purgatory waiting
Waiting to approach, I sink,
I see nothing nothing
To imagine nothing
            Further in the
                Dark parameter still
Still enough room
        To grope with hands
To flagellate your limbs
Slightly.) WHAT HEAVEN IS.
  A circumferential institution
Spacious seemd lamina
Reachable entrance strobes
On again off again the HOLE
Opens and closes
And one day it opend
And thrown out was humanity
            Before it closd,
And kept out from
Creation were the faces
Of perfect minds

(Waves consuming rock,
The providence of ocean veils itself behind
                    The gameplay of a lawless
Element—therein dwells the MYSTERY.
Contained in the plashing of the blue then quick
Tableau—of plashing blue—
                —Screams secretly,
An instant that at first is blamed on a literary pause
In the action—for the sake of dramatic affect. But perhaps
Life has paused. The affliction of reality is then deprived
                The spleen of motion, by becoming an image. But
then,
Another instant quoted here: the splashing drives the blue to
ivory by
This queer alchemy of NATURE—

And ivory to ectoplasm spread
Across, that sheens, the splintered rock,
Leaving there a providence so lamed
—That by phonetic surf does hiss and
Heel like an animal impacted.)

SECOND TRY. Into chaos whatever rings
        Is vaulted back,
To the place where sounds
Are things, and things retract.

(The ringing noise is
Jettisoned out forward
By the Fulcrum balancing
The mental and physical)

The rest, lost forever

In abyssal middles scripture
    Passed off as accrued mythology
Over the years over eons of ages
Some aberrant dysplasia of beliefs
—Beliefs made hushed bashful by chaos gasped
                Out of lore, so that it may not
Be lore but fact that took awhile
To be fact fraught to conflate the rest
With the whole and still
This religion of pieces
Protract the essences
        To a messy distillation

By the rights of their own
Sentience left to unravel
As the pitch is cracked,
 And the proof of a voice
    Having been a voice that
Spoke this text is made
Made a fact that
    Physically exists

    So that Nothing need exist
Any more, nothing does,
And everything that did
    Is in a little WORLD of bust

It is the place where
        The source is mimicked,
And the mimicry replaced—
        The vanquished Aleph
            Is dead—lying like a spud
    In impotent space—this is a place
Where thought is stone

And noise punctures a spelling
Wound wound across sound
Yet never quite getting through
—Angering for emancipation
From the stoic of these hazard
          Walls—vocal moieties—
        Thought counted again, as grains
Of dust, the beans that slide
      Across the abacus

The prickle of bacterium …
   The wound is close to being healed
             But then a rushing of meaning
Summoned Solid and to bleeding
The quaver of rich voices
      From throats itching travel
On the lathe froth: of richer truth:

Looking up at the
Sempiternal turning of the perpetual masque—

      To orange an evening
Moon goes: the face of—
Which is Markd and deepend by
 The pummeling of craters, obviously, look up,
See the fender of psyche wash down the scintillate edicts of
Our scandals sent like down
A swathe of sendal.

Wash out like the moon wept
      Back to us the pains below
  In dying trash had we sneezed upwards
Our wishing Minerals, into stars into things
—Of the sky all in wishing

94

Pieces that when
Arrived to pock the moon will writhe,
          Writhe and suffocate under the dusk

In their turn will turn ugly and
Posthumously disintegrate
Due to the unforgiving pelt of those-
-Large astral carbons
That we, too, creatd in anger, rather, for
          The MOON to unwillingly foster,
        Hoping for a phantom hope
To be offerd by a circle that
          Seems not to suffer ever

No whole inhabits
The sky, no one
Soul for the disparagd

Have we lookd upwards
          At this upturnd shadow of-
 -Structureless of eternal peripheral,
And have seen a big manila hole
          That, amidst the lost ambiguity
Of callous apathetic space
          Seems not so negligible

It is no use, alas,

He has found hope in
BLUE Nothingness JUST

BECAUSE: speak of water: FOG say:
Well: I give essence extra to
          The essences

      And bless that which toils
Only in communion never the
      Quid pro quo with nature—
One thing one rock smoothd into sand over time grown ancient
and
 Sand bequeathd to the pulmonary rise
And consignd fall of the
Water whose face to the air speckd
By an observing sun breathing photosynthesis
      Without the feeling need for reciprocation
       Yet and is it reciprocated the moist backwash
      Clutterd foam rushd
Between spissiond families of rock lending itself, to itself, the
roar
      Of nature in her musing giveth
All to all the riches, as of old old
  Stones bigger into stones than
Themselves, simplicity in them
      Older than creation—
      Everything is in simultaneous exchange
       For everything—the currency
     Of nature is in the humid air
  The charmd buzzing sound found
  In the onomatopoeia of birdsong,
      Cheeping quaqua in the bush,
And the skelter thirsting of the rove wave,

While humans lackey humans
    Go tit for the tat,
While humans lackey humans
Who fail, and they try
Again

The human contravening of

Circles that bail out into
Tangents of squares, making us all the
More confusd, and then while
This is in something rotting
By the pairing of unnatural
Transports in order to
Station each individual eternally
In the same meld, the
Scheme of nature profits
By prodigious propitiates of oneness
That though rememberd by the
Psalms of weed and flower
Retain a different power after the fact
And will still by the jargon of
Humans seem feeble and
Forgotten, and yet nature
In snapping to—will immediately
Undervalue the tragedy of
Human struggle to folly forever
At what the natural WORLD around us
May blithe run on a spool,
And drop the translucent
Knitting without thinking
Twice:

There is a feeling I have
Felt. It is
Puny and focused,
A louse feasting
Upon my temperament

The Explosion of
The myth into existence
So suddenly it is not

A myth, was never a myth, was the—
Unification of split results
 Into an emulsion of the whole,
Which when splitting had the
Components gone scattered
Between space,
Giving them the illusion
—Of not being there

Everything is then slowly obtained.
A fresher kerf of the same wood
        By an axe hacking opposite rifts
Into the Timber multiple
                Routes to the same limbo

 Belting sonic—locusts
In swarm—
A notation of the din
Is made is then
Disappeared from the mind,
I sway in resting sensing—hums

In my jaw—cold, childish
                Motives and suspicions,
Dark characters effusing
 Darkness however found clearly
Like dust in the sun, these,
My family, and friends

The environment acquiring a
  —Spare exhaustion onerous
Colors that weigh on the eye,
Robbing thinning nerves
—Of thinning feel flowing leaving

Nothing beneficial behind
 And instigating the release of
A resinous mixture
Intruding from the ducts

—This prolonged wave steep
Wake at top then the
Body curves itself beneath
Itself the
Storming of
Darkness—visible—weltering
CEREBELLUM—welling—

—In ethyl eyes—heart beating in
 Pulsing, in tandem with
The heaving pressure of these secretions—the
Diverse taxonomy of human
   Human frailties: this new etymological
Growth out from the ocular rim,
These are words as tears,
Down running in liquid roots
 Neither described as Greek or-
       -Roman and the seed yet is in the same
Soil of language

I am in awe of the profound strategy
Made, in the herding of
Locusts, much as the herding
—Of the universe—together—

I discover in sadness the structural
Semblable between sadness between
 And everything else,
Two codes ulterior one

To the other of which is realized
Somewhere else but sprouting
Each from the Stuff of amazement the
Greener stuff, I am in
Awe of how
Easily expand the demarcations

There are layers to the
Biology of speech, they perhaps-
-The patterned moniliform that pad
The ground, blindly, feeling
        For symbols
That cease not to grow
When they are found, and even more when,
When they are experienced,
 No relief to the priking of the
Stamens of a nerve it was
A different sort of grief—

—The chattering of my teeth,
 A main is scooped out.
I garrote my psyche
Like a butcher:

Our hearts on the slab, awaiting, a prime cut.
We faction but a peep of intellect
To our benevolent heads
While closet spectrums rummage through
Our fossilized synapses. They try to make a fire from the stone.
        The fresher nerves that pulp our brain
Are parts that do not recognize, their whole
—And hoard the trim dexterity possessed by pointing
Only—at one solitary flow, of thought—that
    Scuttles on—a peremptory train:

A boy is born: and all he knows
        Is all the WORLD could know—however,
            The boy knows nothing of his gift:
        The Infant: he has his thrifty concepts
            Of himself and how his W0RLD
            May shift:

Because to shape the clay of wits—takes the wallowed
                Resonance: years and time
            To let the mind work out
                The fits:
        The jazzy wisdoms of the juvenile, puerile, conjured
            From a core purpose: and
        Chimerical razz, are what the
JUVENILE struggles to see
        And only sees a bit—before
The mind sits—
And as adults we poor things, we focus on the bits—

And what they see is FOG
—Like eyes over the tall fence—is
The very pith of innocence
Trying to choke young
Minds with drink—to overflow the gourd
                But time morphs every understanding
From big ideology, into a sensibility, of better economy
And so thus turns the vernal bloat of thought
On the gyre of niggard reasoning.
And turning our heads upon our heads
Is the new wave of adulthood, which
—Which becomes mundane. The boy,
        The infant's little hands cannot
            Yet shape an EARTH of Intellect

    But rather he quickly tows his mass across whatever
knowledge
    He might witness—
        And harvests just a crumb from
            The great evening's light: the great wash: of what
            He knows within:

    And my last thought ran up the dyke
        And straight through the gnash of cane
        Infernal thicket clotted vine and my last naked
—Spazzing crazy through fertile wet roots vertical,
Vertical growths. Thick weeds thrash out forest
Threshold old just much—

—As what will lay all
Before the last tock of minutes—
He dared each turn, frightened and, and
        Ballsy in the human perils
Of a redoubt that implodes
  With each step fervently
  Through this monotony
—Of the fifth element, never before
Believing in himself as he did
  Then, when engrossed in
The creeping harmonies
—Of a closet death in every bite of the thorn and split
  Of the bone—he is born from the
Climax of rarified beasts wailing out
  From corrupt breath feeling the aching
Tooth of blood through gums aching
Panic of the hunt and

Back aways
  The first arrived where

It had started again,
        The mildew of stress caught,
An odor, his eyes clouded
And haunted,
Opaque in the plaque of violence
            Driven like a bad stain throughout
The shaking span: of his reason:
Which I, being that, left him alone
 With on the dyke.

I stopped to look at him, he had
            Become a beast of ripped flesh
Assorted pieces from the edge
 Of some universal apathy
 And pledged in a living blot
Thronged that is in threnody together
—From happy throats, out that lace
 The wrongs, tame the Bitch and
Ever wronging took the right to another
Level of dead sounds,
Impossible to render, harmonies fight
With abrasive phonic violence—

Fewer wronging all made right when
        Looked at. An obtuse declension of even
The most superb cognizance is caused
In how it hastens to point out the Ratio
 —Of wrongs favorable to rights
            Nearly out of some infernal lassitude
So that the fewer wrongs are overruled
By a perturbed colossus of right things
 A fortiori some oversight, default of averages,
        Give me guilt, and I will make it nothing

With my choir wrong everyday!,
This in turn will be something that
Does not exist but in nutty fucking Realms,
        You know,
                    Things chaotic things clutter of
                    Voices banging against the finish of the sky

Sky air air whirred rapture of the billions in the choir
Hang as reductive pictures in this vermillion
Antechamber: couch the sound there in simulacrums,
            Blind elements, for once. This art is
    Cogitations lacking

Anything amazing in the verge that connects the
Disintegration to no deep
    Speaker merely a loud nothing that
                    Sinks I have no dispute, with—pruned cad
—Cad of a Catechist yet and is it an original
Fasting of the mind, I am
Absolved, no need for Baptismal

To be in want of an idea, is a depiction of anxiety,
—Having truth only
In its most formative ways
And seeing blackness in the logic
That is finished to a point and
                    Cannot be finished further,
And so written is the sky
                And written is the air,
                And despair is in the perception
            —Of both that are the same and yet
        Not able to be fully seen
            Or Understood:—

. ..   .

Prologue:

Ewrhm,
Enacted to act without
Proper redaction
The retraction of words
To minimalism

Disject the phrase
And the power
Grows in pieces

The further elaborated
    Meaning of the poem
Makes things smaller.
Saturated in extraneous
Charms

The malaise of a bootleg feel
 —As of one who's grown from clouds, dejected,
A description here: of what
Refuses to be described yet.

Chapter One:

  But the form that is calm,
And cool, quiets the beating
    Spasm contraction of the muscles,

Which tighten, around the consequence,
Something tussled into relevance
By purely an improvised eminence

Tussled
By the grand wind of life that
Still merely releases wind
Upon a page to dash clouds, expecting
The whisper to conjure
Up an inspiration

Bootless creative endeavors
    Then left to spike fuzz and
Spoil in malingering stuff,
Clever words cleave themselves
    As of dough for bread—

The soft-shoeing of formative
            Diction hitching ridden
Plot—I shall amble, with a limp,
Ever towards place,
Arriving at forged place

I attempt to dissuade the
Inevitable or evade the promising
Junctures leading me there
And I come up in my own cleanly

Chapter Two:

    But shall I skip the climax
And degrade like out the blip
—Of traveling particles?
Loss of dynamic in the drawl fusiform draw
        —Of neurons and electrons
Struggling to merge—

So I wait and go about
My day waiting for the action
To rise and shall sight
My downfall soon, just as
One recalls, when in
The presence of Saint Peter
The Files of each
Step in life that brought them
To the end of wax

My father
Is said to have asked me
Why I thought myself caged
And I, knowing the
Conversation did not exist,
Stated that I knew I was caged
Because I could not feel
The bars

The momentary cloud of dreams

My noble, frank being …
            Prohibits me from making
    The glib cut, the first incision
          Is the most problematic.
        The inception of an infant path
That in the blear of possibility
Could lead much to
Destruction, as to perfection

No fast stitch, no breaking
Point, always the low pitch of
Zephyr rattling these frames

—Of myself and not forgotten not till
         I nod off—
              I connect the dots
Without being connected to
         The dots. They make
Themselves a way
              —Beyond me. Into
The single flare
Of light out from
Shadow far
Away. And as
It closes in,
         I wait
For the closure knowing
No other flare will come,
Only another line
Of dots, only another
Passage
Into the ether:
 I will start as a
Sphere, no, a
 Pit—a pit inside
Which an atom
Lingers, a single
 Atom loafing
In the darkness,
   Unused—till one
Day splitting into
Spheres that Double and
Triple and Grow, within the depths
Until the moment
         —Comes when the
Force of all it overwhelms
Terminal space. Forever cherish the

First fission, it was
Perfect back then
A perfect circle I start as
        A circle. I dive
Into pit picking out legs and arms they
        Lay in a Heap at the bottom
            Like the limbs of discarded
 Mannequins. Longing to put them together,
They remain separate, the chance
 For unity is gone thus the circle
            Becomes imperfect, as would
A machine left to swing its wheels out
        Out of place after too much
 Time turning disjunct
    Line drawn round and
Round and round-
 -Again never but
Perfect roundness only
 Once, when the pattern peaks,
And again in dimensions
Off our own plateau,
 A part still of which
        Contains in us
        Hopefully

        No alternative
 To this, I know scenes
    In my head—if like there
Is one, I know images
        Or perhaps scenes—of what
I should be. Many levels
To go many deepening rings
Round the stalactite
        And with that metaphor—

The thought of this all
Becomes like it had
Before, rather it is a cave
Instead but the same negative space,
 The same need to rally-
-Against perceived forces that all the same amount to
                    Nothing. Absolutely
          Nothing. Less madness
Less madness,
Experience of guilt
For the toys of our marginal past
And onwards future

I try to summon a
Spirit of intensity
I find I
Cannot get there—
This feeling of
No feeling—frequently has
Been the host of my
Thoughts—

I watch, thin
—Thin scope of
My witching sight—the days
And reactions pass
          Over in sections—I have
      The audacity to say
That time has passed I am

   Frozen in time. Time
  Does not pass.
  I am left rooted firmly left-
      -To bud the black buds of former

Let us say, they are the
—Predilections of
          Some notorious thing, moving,
  Moving—in the streets of
     Scrupled thought—

Time has stopped
To rest on the azimuth on the
Quarter of a the the the
—Of a tangent refusing
To perform
Another second another
Learned moment. So, then: I begin again at
The beginning: with
     A different start
Than at before, I
Have known for
          Such a long time
Of my downfall
Although every way
I began started
Differently always
          Ended up useless
And as pitiable as damp coals,
And will return once
Again to putrefaction,
Yet and I see it
As the same—
I know such a thing the
Same, as when living I had
So many years ago

     My apostles have waited
And are now established

Themselves, grown bloated
With inactivity
All the faith shrunken
To menopause
Brought on by the fictitious
Possibility that has worn
          Our structures down into
Things truly gothic

          Never bothered to examine
    Again, only forgotten
Until approached briefly
    And we felt around for
Loose spirits.
      We are ever haunted
              By the bones of
    Sublime things)

    The junk of my past …
Heating in the compost are
Cruelties stalking
    My peace of muted mind
I wish for it to stay mute

Mind that sees no
 Difference in trifles
      Between, and large errors
          Committed by a
      —Sultan of the Bad
Benignly wrapping
His turban up imploring
      For redemption, from the
Cell where stinks it
In concealed trash

    I have Conscience that taps
The same key for foibles
And for horrors,
Failing to distill a median
Of anguish

Would be illumined dimly
In the day, I prefer it to reduce
In the night's obligatory
 Portent. Not ever any to be
Shown in their tragedy, exposed by the day, never,
 There is no day in them, not even
An ebbing gown of futile purple
That punctures the twilight
And expands into dulling strings
           Like ink in water,
   My horrors I make more oblique
      As they reveal more plainly,
More and more and more plainly
 The extent of the damage each
Carnage had caused

The blind have more resilience
        To their senses—hijack the power,
The power of a removed normalcy
And lugging it to another sense,
    Strengthening smell or taste or feel,

While belies my nose the whiff of some deceit
In the pollen particles of roses
 Odors that are discordant with the feel
There should be flowers
That smell of feet

. ..   .

(Being in the pith of mirth
I sought to comprehend my worth
      And talked in a vein most clearly vain
To those who could not
            Appreciate the pain)

. ..   .

(There's a touch of you I think I can fear
—The smile suffers in it, the leer
Becomes it soft the most I get
 From you—the press of phobic fealty,
Feigning some abrasive motto
That catches on a sneer between the lips
A required trust based on some canonical
 List of laws, regarding human relationships
For YOU not something automatic,
      —Stupid grouch—
—Stick in the mud—
One to another, we are close but stiff—

One sees an edge that lopes out the cliff
Of your dry brokenness
—A larking imminence projecting further—
Perceived as maudlin sprees of troubled shadow
Across your narrow furtive seeking brow
      And daunting features already flaccid
As the blank shell of a dead crustacean.
                  An expanse of pretense haunts bespeaks
   Your own adulterated sense of what is credence,
A percussive skepticism of intentions

Based on all that one can stand as loss
—That sometime lapse the shield into dross
        And shows YOU have a lot to learn.

Your modal expressions struggle to seem kind,
        As if some creature concept were forlorn
To be addressed, although the recreant mind
        Might tickle in the center of your craving
Only to be pushed back down, although
YOU hide nothing—blatant, a clown—
        And vent an outward humor, inward scorn—
    At times, YOU think that life cannot be born
But be built must, like bridges over thought
        —The delinquent moil of restrained ideas—
Which grow to live the pang deeper,
            They whimper from the stream that feels
        Beneath, wheels
        Beneath—bridge. A sublime
            Stream, manipulated by the coarse
    Yet bated transit
    —Of wind in panic, and YOU
Try and cross the bridge ...

But, then, the grief begins to spoil in spite,
And this gross necrolatry
    Of the past in passing
            Should only the demeanor meaner make.
And seeming anguish that compels one to
        Feel something seeming fake, is something done
 By something, more acute than YOU can muster
Power enuff against to repulse what shall become
A serial delirium. Muzzle the apocryphal,
        The apocryphal nature of assertions
        As to the shapely quality of your character

—Of character that YOU possess unrivaled
In explicit temerity never bridled, once—
        So that the timid fraud that pulses in your face
                Might not plainly
Be observable,
Still, this covering
Of YOU—is gamble—
        You murmur wry recalcitrance vexed and
Still these things reveal themselves in specks

The small mechanics of your menace
Ascribe to modicum the chimaera in modicum, upon that face,
Atomic, nearly, once are blithe, that is; and in the running fable
                —Of life that alters ever from sincerity,
There is the change, often not foretold
        And yet it happens, as one grows old
—In first the ripe conscience lacking security
            Surrenders the chromatic flush of imagining
And the dew that films your eyes, communicant
        Of a more salient honesty, comes
To dry, and dry, and dry and dry—
When staking merit on the return of looks
        YOU do not service well, and learn to hate-
                -Which in turn, comes to be, a comfortable platitude.

Done all for the sake, of attaining—HAVEN—that are rotten—
            Security is much the style of delusion: that fools
                The judgment of a man, as to the fossils of his
attitudes,
His ends and his beginnings, and his accomplishments,
    Obliging each with tinctures of mythy greatness
            Yet times there are when honesty is cinched
            Before the loom of expression can pretend, that
No faculty has gone missing from the clench,

So, then, the honesty, though unfinished, is there—
—Is expressed, in the stead of a false whole
And as spoken is equally in eloquence—
I know that obsessive analysis has a price
That, without rest should soon
Grow tired of this testing,
This fulsome palaver with himself
Himself grown fetid repulsive cadaverous,
That inner shaking of a convulsive mind
The harping missives, in his gut
Cannot find peace, in a rut-
-His own making.)

The amount of experience
I wished to cultivate over ruts though:
Time and time the way
Out of knowing—ah—time,
So much taken from me
In minutes of scorn and
Hours of unrest, alone,
Unborn years stuck in erasure
Time after time until no time
I live in no time.
The paradigm is shifted leave my watch to
Thread the measure of learned
Life, I am ever in doubt
—Of the true spirit in MAN
That compels the ticker

Like a watch, I must
Be wound up spiritless
And dumb to the foundation
As patients of Asperger

Unperturbed, I wished to
  Pursue the venues
Most alien, and personal—
To discover what
Drives the valves open, for
          Everyone else,
And closes them, for everyone
        Else to exclude the
            Stale exponents mortified
          Blood—pushed back all those years and now
  Brought forward—in
And out of the pump—as such I knew
I must learn how to think
      Or else my blood
Shall become weak
Unedited

I had gone all my life
    Without thinking. It
Did not occur to me to
        —String my visual narrative
  Into a sightless derision
    Of verbs and nouns.

If only, I wonder if

          Only. I seek such
      Understanding sorely,
    My gut aches with regret
At not having sooner
    Relinquished the err
      Of my presumptions
    As to what was normal,
        What doing, was normal

Why had I not bothered
Before to think on the
    Same plane as what
Was normal questionmark

I have in some way
        Thought before, mostly,
I do not know what it is—
    It could be thinking, perhaps
  Not. I guess one could say
I have rendered all thought
In simultaneous bronze plates,
As Blake engraved the
    Experience of his Innocence

I do not localize my
Cogitations, my questions
        And answers and every
Contemplation, seems
        Snared in a state of déjà vu
They do but come to me
As faces peering through
  That before had exhibited
Themselves—

—Watching me
Grow in my MOTHER's
Abdomen,
They are captured
In solution of difficult
  Nuclei in yet an
        Embryonic form

    All the answers
      They eye me over then
Collapse out of my
    Natal vision. They return
Years after to perform
       The old ritual, the old
     Pistons bursting steam
And before I know it
      The deed is already
   Done, had been done
Years ago and was
Repeating, in neglect
    —Of new time

The deed is done,
Without my having to
Derive a sense of sense
   Out of this phenomenal
Utility

I think sometimes in
Senses, like the smell
Of fungus and
Mildew in the wood after
Hard rain,
That reminds me of my
Uncle's glasses, they would
Fog up:

I think sometimes in
   Hypothetical situations playing
Between myself and
Someone else. The
Forgiven the stooly the

Jackass the duly
Appreciated
Receive display,
   In images of
     Deification fractured confused

    The men and women
I talk to in my brain
Speak
     In shades and motions
 I too speak
   In motions and shades
And no words need
  Be said to understand
  The consequence

How I think, if it can be
    Called that. It is not a simple
Explanation—there is a
Wide margin of error
Involved in displacing the fastidious
Guiding hand
Of Power that examines
Those Compartments of
My riddled figuring

—Ranking in the seat of inference
     Are words single words …
Seen white against black
   Space, conveying some
   Beleaguered importance
In their catatonia—

—The hand grasps my spine,

    Realizing that it will be removed,
I must let go the cataclysm,
Mess of chaos this, dutiful suck this,
               —Thoughts—
To my disappointment
They become burnished outwardly
    As speech speaking but echoes,
The trance of an iron head,

Of it all warps, stricken
From the record of the strophes
Perhaps is there some
Collusion of ciphers upstairs
    To reap the mistakes
Made in the triangulation
Of what is thought
And what in the mind spoken-
    -To simmers like
    The last dwindle of
An ember before
Dying out

    Denied the even
Most cautious last
Burn before emancipated
    To other more fatuous
   WORLD: fatuous, indeed,
That is what awaits him—
    A WORLD in the middle
Conquered by GOD,
Prosaic hegemony ultimately
Vapid

A Serengeti of

        Taciturn blankness
Reveals over a face
Hollowed with fatigue
        As things become harder
And harder to do—the bodily
Delay of the nervous
System—those in steady
        Convergence with death,
Meeting finally at
A punctual stillness

Beforehand he knows his pain
        And the gratuitous nature
—Of its many recessions and arrivals,
And struggles to style upon his face
        The pure verity of all this shit by using
            The mute signals of
                Expression, having by now mostly
            Lost the ability to speak at length.
        And even this late in the game,
            Discovers he does not have
            The strength, as yet,
To look a man of pain,
And never could he
Seem a man of pain,
A man dying thinks simply.

He grows frustrated with
The endless experimentation
To distill his face into
Something truly evocative
—Of torture,
But it is the same sneer out
        Upon his pathetic World

—Of pathetic solaces
Retold in the same
    Anguishing silent drag
Up and down Face,
The functions of
Jaw and Eyebrow, a toil

Feelings are lonely
They desire company
Rosebud, he whispers,
Pursed lips in agony
To enunciate enough
To echo a little into
Xanadu, decreed the stately
Pleasure dome—
All is gone of it,
No lasting odor of pastille,
    No fresh wind to stalk
    These festooned chambers of Dust and of Doubt,
Childhood Anno Domini

And we,
Crooning sentiments,
Do not indulge our eyes enough
        To find the foggy playing of figures
        And patterns, jumping past
                His ghost, before
        The death, so close
It breathes, that one
  Can hear the hearse,
But these figures are
Not yet quite
Desiccated, nor cracked,
        They are the phantoms

Of guileless memory

Such finely calculated damage,
How horrifying. Slowly over the careful precision
        Of time, I changed. There is a plan, with difficulty
Found in the tinny ticking of minutes
            Minutes swallowed by the hour
        And the dark plus of hours

Until the lush realities of the present become adumbrations
Of a year that ends upon a vague prolepsis, and the past
                    Becomes to us, a waste of instances

        The clunky order we give to life will doom us
                    To a single judgment of time
One learns a single judgment of time: it is
A duped sensibility based upon assumptions
                    Of a thing that must not be assumed
        That due to the expanse the length of it—
That due to the complete absence of effort-
            -Needed for one second to usurp the one
                    Preceding it—the ease of something
That will always go on—well, in the conflicts
Day and night that transpire
Across our variegated WORLD—I give one example that
            You know, so as to make it easier
For you to understand—in days and nights
                Which go quarreling on in the
Contrasts, as a father
Quarrels with his son about college—such, that transpire
                Across our variegated WORLD
Such ease of such things seems, the product of something
ingenuous

(But it is quite deliberate, pernicious
          —As those spectral perspectives of ourselves
 And time shall drain us all of who we were,
 And now, and then, we are another person
          And know the fact of this beyond denial
                    In the dankest obscurity of mind)

          That skepticism that suspicion
               Of any prolonged spiritual comfort
 Chimmers like a reflex in the brain
               As regards even the cheapest identity
          This is humorous, in a way, as like the idiot
                         Uniquely aware
                    —Of his idiocy
                    And I know only how to alter
          The nature of my limitations-
          -As regards the poem. It has become
 Something of a grey fabric, tousled
 In the weave, in the rickety loom
          —A freakish and bizarre sweater chidden
          From the mouth of psychic heddle.

. .. .

(There was a time, when I checked
My watch, and saw that it was twelve,
I look again and it is ten …

Is there in the hectic speed
Of comprehension certain
Excessive relativities beget
Dyslexia in the selection,

A margin of error, that

Distracts the margins)

I see this woman standing over
    The sink, head slightly
    Ajar
    However, as to what is on her mind
We still cannot readily assume. So we theorize Nakedly
About this woman
    And find her cloistral consciousness
Has sensed our observation. In response it
    Awakens its tongue
Speaks of injustices, as if a plea to us could move us
One cannot put a finger on them
She has waited a long time to be free
    And has not been freed
Began, awhile ago, to shrink her person into externalities
    Like the twittering of her clonus
Noticed, by her busy friends, now tenfold
    After the deduction was made:
Fascination with life as it is
Simply because it is life, is not enough,
But it is at least something—
    —Such is the succor against her pessimism
    Nonetheless makes her nervous,
    She clenches the porcelain berms of the sink
    Unfortunately, she is in general more aware of
pessimism
    Down the chute of the flask
    Is like entering the nave of her discontent
    And the whiskey burns more uniquely, in her throat
Perhaps that is why she keeps on drinking dreads
    —Dreads return to the debacle:
    That unamazing type of burn. She feels
    Her weensy life burning. It is not preferable

She sighs like dead wind

(As if all air were spurious
And wind the distorted clone of its fundament self)

Now:
Contemplating the cinereous offal
        That collects in the ashtray
On the table next to her bed
              Where from the kitchen
     She had seamlessly moved so that
—So that nothing need be elaborated
In terms of sense of place
Of place, besides the simple statement of place
The two different parts of the house
              She had moved one from the other
                    As I have said, seamlessly—

—It were almost fact, that between going
These two images of locations
     She does not fully exist—

Beaten the stuffing from the day.
          The riddle ameliorates
Like her hands over her face.
As she sits like that on the side of the bed
                    This is not enough

D.C DeMarse grew up in New York City. Furthest Agent is his debut collection.

As always thanks for reading.

CPSIA information can be obtained at www.ICGtesting.com
Printed in the USA
BVOW07s1705230415

397225BV00002B/436/P